LIKEWISE. *Go and do.*

A man comes across an ancient enemy, beaten and left for dead. He lifts the wounded man onto the back of a donkey and takes him to an inn to tend to the man's recovery. Jesus tells this story and instructs those who are listening to "go and do likewise."

Likewise books explore a compassionate, active faith lived out in real time. When we're skeptical about the status quo, Likewise books challenge us to create culture responsibly. When we're confused about who we are and what we're supposed to be doing, Likewise books help us listen for God's voice. When we're discouraged by the troubled world we've inherited, Likewise books encourage us to hold onto hope.

In this life we will face challenges that demand our response. Likewise books face those challenges with us so we can act on faith.

likewisebooks.com

LETTERS TO A
FUTURE CHURCH

WORDS OF ENCOURAGEMENT
AND PROPHETIC APPEALS

EDITED BY CHRIS LEWIS

IVP Books

An imprint of InterVarsity Press
Downers Grove, Illinois

InterVarsity Press
P.O. Box 1400, Downers Grove, IL 60515-1426
World Wide Web: www.ivpress.com
E-mail: email@ivpress.com

InterVarsity Press® is the book-publishing division of InterVarsity Christian Fellowship/USA®, a movement of students and faculty active on campus at hundreds of universities, colleges and schools of nursing in the United States of America, and a member movement of the International Fellowship of Evangelical Students. For information about local and regional activities, write Public Relations Dept., InterVarsity Christian Fellowship/USA, 6400 Schroeder Rd., P.O. Box 7895, Madison, WI 53707-7895, or visit the IVCF website at <www.intervarsity.org>.

All Scripture quotations, unless otherwise indicated, are taken from the THE HOLY BIBLE, NEW INTERNATIONAL VERSION®, NIV® Copyright © 1973, 1978, 1984, 2011 by Biblica, Inc.™ Used by permission. All rights reserved worldwide.

While all stories in this book are true, some names and identifying information in this book have been changed to protect the privacy of the individuals involved.

The song "Be the Centre" by Michael Frye is © 1999 Vineyard Songs (UK/EIRE) (PRS). Administered in North America by Music Services. Used by permission. All rights reserved.

Interior design: Beth Hagenberg

Cover design: Cindy Kiple

Images: letter in a mailbox: © Floortje/iStockphoto
      red door with brass mailbox: © SteveStone/iStockphoto
      mailbox: © Björn Magnusson/iStockphoto
      postage stamps and marks: © Matt Knannlein/iStockphoto
      postmarks: © Valerie Loiseleux/iStockphoto

ISBN 978-0-8308-3638-3

Printed in the United States of America ∞

Library of Congress Cataloging-in-Publication Data

Letters to a future church: words of encouragement and prophetic appeals / Chris Lewis, editor.
    p. cm.
  Includes bibliographical references.
  ISBN 978-0-8308-3638-3 (pbk.: alk. paper)
  1. Church. 2. Christianity—Forecasting. 3. Twenty-first
century—Forecasts. I. Lewis, Chris, 1982-
  BV600.3.L48 2012
  269—dc23

                                              2011051589

| P | 18 | 17 | 16 | 15 | 14 | 13 | 12 | 11 | 10 | 9 | 8 | 7 | 6 | 5 | 4 | 3 | 2 | 1 |
| Y | 27 | 26 | 25 | 24 | 23 | 22 | 21 | 20 | 19 | 18 | 17 | 16 | 15 | 14 | 13 | 12 |

Contents

Hope

Preface

Chris Lewis

The story of how *Letters to a Future Church* came to be begins almost six years ago. It was my fourth year of theological studies at Tyndale University College. At 2 a.m., with my roommate fast asleep, I began to follow through on an idea I'd discussed with three friends earlier that week—we needed to organize some kind of event to further discussion around the things we were learning at school that we hadn't even heard about while growing up in the church. Themes deeply woven into the Scriptures, like the kingdom of God and an integrated view of justice, seemed like new material while studying the Gospels together. How had we missed this? Why didn't anyone tell us?

E-mails were sent.

A week later we received our first confirmation from a pastor in Houston whom most people in Toronto wouldn't have known but we agreed that he had something important to contribute. Then came the e-mail that propelled our course ahead. We received word that the church guru du jour we had invited had agreed to come to our event. Our event, mind you, hadn't been thought through or given a name, nor had we even thought about where a budget for such things would emerge.

Meetings ensued.

We needed a name. After a few weeks we settled on Epiphaneia Network, the result of a serendipitous trip down a number of rabbit trails at thesauras.com. *Epiphaneia* is the Greek word for "epiphany," which references a sudden realization of something while also recognizing Epiphany, the holiday in the Christian calendar that celebrates God becoming one of us.

The next five years saw this group of four friends plan five events in Toronto, four of which became known as The Evolving Church conference. As it turns out, the name was a bit problematic for some people—we regularly received e-mails from folks who wondered if we even believed in Jesus. When we responded by indicating that we did believe in Jesus and asked if they wanted to go for coffee and talk about it, we never heard from them again. Weird. Nevertheless, it was apparent that something beautiful was happening as early as our first event, when the president of the university took me aside and explained that he felt like this gathering represented a watershed or a seismic tremor, not only for Tyndale but for the Canadian church.

Our goal always was to foster discussion in the church and ask people to constantly consider and reconsider what Jesus was asking them to be here, today. Along the way we talked about "restoring justice," about a church "amidst the powers" and what it might look like to be a people with a "kingdom economy." Then came an idea for an event like none other we had tried before, and a renewed sense of energy, creative spark and purpose followed.

Eighth Letter took place on October 1-2, 2010, and was based on the book of Revelation, particularly the letters to the seven churches. We invited anyone to submit a letter addressed to the church in North America, which contained the author's most pressing message. If you had one thing to say to the church, we asked, what would it be? For two months we received letters almost daily from authors who obviously loved the church and just wanted to talk things through. We ended up inviting those we knew would have creative and timely messages to the church to share alongside people we had only known through their letter submission.

The highlights for me were watching two friends share their own thoughts at Eighth Letter. One friend's painful journey inside the church seemed to be redeemed before my eyes as it became clear that her story was *our* story. Everyone in attendance agreed that a standing ovation was the only appropriate response. The second highlight came from a masterful piece of music-as-letter by a lifelong friend whose journey with the church has been a vocational dream at best and vitriolic nightmare at worst. If nothing else were to have come of Eighth Letter, all the work would have been worth it to share those moments with friends.

This book, then, is the culmination of those letters presented at Eighth Letter.

Today the four friends remain as such. People have shared with us on more than one occasion that the best way to ruin a friendship is to go into business together—we're living proof that the opposite is true: The best way to stay connected, we maintain, is to do something you believe in together, holding tightly to the thing you're trying accomplish while loosening your grip around the idea that finances and numbers are always the primary indicator of success.

When I think back over the last few years of working at Epiphaneia with Nathan Colquhoun, Steve Cox and Darryl Silvestri, I cherish all the hours of meeting together, the preparation and the kingdom dreaming. This book is the result of God's hand on our hard work together, and I'm pleased beyond words that we get to share this together and that all of those hours of work can somehow live on through this project.

On behalf of Epiphaneia.

Introduction

Andy Crouch

On my daughter's eleventh birthday a truly miraculous item came through our mail slot—a two-page handwritten letter from a fourteen-year-old friend of her brother's who had heard about her birthday and decided to send some cheerful congratulations. The whole family crowded around the strange artifact, hand-addressed in a teenage girl's reverse-slanting print, marveling at the generosity and spontaneity and total unlikelihood of such a gesture. I believe it was the only handwritten letter that came to any member of our family that month. E-mails? Facebook messages? Texts? Tweets? We've got plenty of those, a deluge not unlike the piles of letters that start arriving at number four, Privet Drive, to invite Harry Potter to Hogwarts, wriggling their way in through the windows and the fireplace— or, to pick a sadder and more apt comparison, multiplying like the sorcerer's apprentice's brooms, overwhelming us with their insistent out-of-control helpfulness. We're drowning in communication. But we're starved for letters.

A letter, it seems to me, requires one crucial quality that few electronic messages attain: an old-fashioned word, *consideration*. Writing a letter is an act of considering. Letters require pausing, contemplating, stopping whatever else we are doing and making ourselves available to consider—to consider an occasion (a birthday, an achievement, a loss, a visit, a gift); to consider the one to whom we are writing, almost always dear to us in some way but also always, like all those dear to us, an enduring mystery; to consider the distance between us and the reasons for that distance (travel, career, adventure, leaving one and cleaving to another, estrangement, imprisonment, war); and then finally to consider how to bridge that distance, on this occasion, with some token of our love and with the truth.

Perhaps the most spectacular letter in Scripture is the Apocalypse of John, also known as the book of Revelation—hardly a conventional letter then or now, but very clearly conceived and addressed as such. The aging apostle, we know, was in exile on the parched and lonely island of Patmos, which even today only survives thanks to the regular visits of tankers bearing potable water—who knows how John and the sparse population of that day managed on that bit of rock in the middle of the Aegean, surrounded by beauty you could neither eat nor drink. He had plenty of time to consider. One thing he apparently never stopped considering was the rhythm of the Christian week of worship, for he begins his letter by telling his far-flung readers that he had been "in the Spirit on the Lord's day." Though the whole point of exile was surely to keep this apostle far from any church, that Sunday morning John was indeed in church, and the church was on his mind.

The whole Apocalypse is a letter, the report of what John saw in the Spirit as he was worshiping right along with the other fledgling Christian communities around the Mediterranean rim—a vision as fantastic then as it is now of the bloody turmoil of the world and the eventual triumph of the King of kings and Lord of lords. A vision that turned upside down everything anyone in the Roman Empire knew to be true; a vision that offered hope to those, like John, who clung to life at the world's most precarious edges and who hoped that their witness to the unlikely Lord Jesus was not in vain.

Before this all unfolds, however, we first encounter some mini-letters—specific and brief addresses to the seven churches scattered around the rim of the Middle-Earth Sea. Like most letters, they have a certain form and structure—each is addressed, for example, not to the church itself but to its "angel," the messenger charged with bringing the words of the Spirit to that church from its Lord. Each concludes with a promise of cosmic scale—"to the one who conquers I will also give the morning star." But despite their similarities of form, these are not form letters. They are highly individual and give due consideration to the strengths and the failings of each community. Some are addressed in warm tones; others offer urgent encouragement in the face of mortal fear; and several, like the warning of impending expectoration to hapless, lukewarm Laodicea, remind us that the One who speaks not only has hair like blazing wool and eyes like flame, but a mouth from which comes a sword.

These letters-within-the-letter help orient us for the disorienting tumult that comes later. They sum up the church in John's time and in ours—faithful beyond measure in some places, mediocre and in disarray in others. They encapsulate the whole message of the apocalyptic genre, which is that things are much better, and much worse, than they seem. Apocalyptic literature breaks into our world to say that the seemingly routine humdrum of the world's workings and the seemingly predictable weekly ritual of worship in fact conceal untold blessings and untold bane. Sooner or later, promises the apocalyptic letter, that which is hidden will be revealed, and it will be far more glorious and far more terrible than we imagined—unless our imagination itself is shaped by the Spirit. And what is true about the whole world is also true about the church—it is better and worse than anyone could ever conceive.

All this is what the aging apostle considered, and wrote down, and circulated to the churches of his time, the frail parchment making its way around the rim of the known world—the letter to end all letters, a letter that has comforted and confounded Christians ever since. Surely it is no great surprise that our canon of sixty-six books ends with a letter. For the witness of the Bible is that the Creator of this vast universe has considered us, has addressed himself to us, has personally brought us the good news that we are remembered, judged, forgiven and saved. So his servants reply: "Maranatha!" Come home, Lord Jesus, to your beautiful, broken world, and make all things new.

In October 2010 a crew no less motley than John's original audience gathered in Toronto for a conference called Eighth Letter. The premise was simple: to invite all sorts of Christ followers to pen their own brief letter to the church. The two particular pieces of genius in that premise were the "brief" part and the "all sorts" part. No presentation was more than fifteen minutes long (a welcome trend in many church conferences, I have to say). And the presenters themselves were not just people who regularly wear the Wireless Headset of Authority at church conferences, but also included several who had submitted essays online that caught the attention of the conference organizers with their passion, clarity and creativity. Indeed, the one and only "letter" that prompted a wholehearted standing ovation was the work of someone almost no one in the room had heard of before that afternoon. You'll get to read that letter, along with many others, in this collection.

I have to confess I was skeptical about how well all of this would go. There are a few significant differences between everyone in this volume and John on Patmos, let alone Jesus himself, who, after all, claimed authorship of the seven letters to the seven churches. We do not walk among the seven lamp stands, nor have we poured out a lifetime in apostolic leadership culminating in a witness's exile at the empire's edge—this was a very ordinary group, from the most well-known to the least. No one claimed authority to unfold scrolls about the true trajectory of things in heaven or earth. Who are we to write letters to the church, whether present or future?

There were some crucial differences too between Jesus' letters and ours—at least the ones I was afraid would be written and presented. Jesus addressed seven specific communities, gatherings of Christians with particular names in particular cities at particular times. We, on the other hand, could easily indulge ourselves in addressing some abstract "church"—not the church in Toronto, let alone the church in York Mills or Corktown; not the church in Los Angeles, let alone the church in Compton or Eagle Rock. Instead we could fashion an imaginary "church" (probably bearing a resemblance to a particular church we had especially loved or loathed or both) and write a letter to that notional community—which of course would not be a proper letter, with its consideration of people and place and story and future, but simply a convenient pretext for an essay about what is wrong or right in whatever we imagine "North American Christianity" to be.

I worried that our letters would partake of all the weaknesses of the "open letter" genre, in which a frustrated pundit or columnist or activist writes a letter to a public figure who seems beyond actual influence, publishing it for general reading (sometimes skipping altogether the step of sending the letter to the ostensible recipient) in hopes of generating public pressure for choices the person addressed would never make on her or his own. Were we going to spend a weekend engaging in that kind of abstract and distant criticism of Christians or Christian institutions somewhere else without knowing their names, their histories, their very particular realities? In other words, were we there to *consider*, to give real consideration not only to our insights but to the people we were addressing? Or were we there to vent our (no doubt numerous and legitimate) frustrations with what goes by the name of "church" in our day, without matching that frustration—which Jesus clearly shares in a number of his own mini-letters—with Jesus' utter commitment to and self-giving for the very communities that disappoint us? And would there be any moments corresponding to the blessings of Jesus' letters, his assurances to fearful and scattered followers (many of them soon-to-be martyrs) that they would eat from the tree of life in the paradise of God, that they would not be harmed by the second death, that one day they would find pressed in their palm a white stone with their true name?

I won't say that my fears were completely unfounded. There were moments of easy generalization (based on real experiences, no doubt) about one or another weakness of "the church"; there were moments of too readily assuming the prophetic mantle to confess others' sins. Somehow it's easier, seeking to make the most of your fifteen minutes, to be incisively critical than to be generously hopeful.

Yet for the most part the letters that weekend exemplified the consideration we all hope for when we open an envelope. They were crafted out of love, thought, pain and prayer. The weekend was a reminder of the energy that has been unleashed in the world by the proclamation of the good news—the sheer variety and beauty of the people who have found themselves captivated by the gospel, embodied as it is in the flawed vessel of the church, and have devoted their lives to helping the church recognize, claim and live up to the message it proclaims.

You can imagine the nervous anticipation that must have

hovered over the rooms where John's spectacular letter was first read as those little communities in Ephesus, Smyrna, Pergamum and the other cities realized that they were being directly addressed by the "voice like many waters." Being human just like us, surely they cringed with embarrassment or flushed with pride as their faults or faithfulness were named; surely they relaxed just a bit with relief, if not schadenfreude, when another community was on the receiving end of the sword of Jesus' mouth.

I suppose the letters in this book will produce similar reactions in us. Some will make us feel all over again the rush of gratitude we experienced when we saw the church at its best at a crucial moment; others will raise to a sharp point the pain of others' failures and our own. And still others will not sound like they are addressed to us at all, because they are not—they are for another part of Jesus' people, and the rest of us just need to listen carefully and pray for our sisters and brothers. Since these letters are not, after all, from Jesus himself, a few may in fact miss the mark entirely, something that will only become clear with much patience, prayer and time.

But all these letters, even the misdirected ones, can be helpful to us. They can sharpen our senses, cause us to sit up a bit straighter and prompt us to listen more intently for the One who truly has addressed himself to us and who will one day return to his bride. "Let anyone who has an ear listen to what the Spirit is saying to the churches."

You Had Me at Hello

Janell Anema

I sat down in July 2010 to write a letter to the twenty-first-century church in North America. The words simply tumbled onto the page.

Dear Church,

I love you. You had me at hello. You are the wind beneath my wings. I'll never let go, Church, I'll never let go. Even as we collide into the icebergs of postmodernity, of hyper-seeker-sensitivity and of moral failure, I'll never let go. While the praise band serenades our submersion into culture, on this ship that might be sinking, I'll never let go.

I quickly realized that my letter was more an homage to *Titanic* than an address to the church, and perhaps that culture ship was already at the bottom of the sea. As suddenly as the words had poured out, the well of prose ran dry. Who was I to address the church? By what inspiration and by whose authority could I write? Surely not by James Cameron's. Instead of pressing forward, I decided to go back to the very beginning— a very good place to start.

My first memories of church are fuzzy and kind of itchy. Fuzzy in that they happened while I was so young, and itchy because

I'm sure I was wearing tights. I was so excited the morning that
my stockinged feet finally reached the wooden pew in front of
me and I stuck my tiny toes into the Communion cup holders.
My memories are blanketed in stained-glass light and animated
across felt boards. In church I was introduced to Jesus and taught
to love him: the Jesus with a lamb across his shoulders, the Jesus
with deep blue eyes, the Jesus with soft brown hair.

I loved that Jesus. And I loved you, church, even then. You
truly had me at hello.

So instead of writing a new letter, I compiled pieces from the
journals of my youth. It turns out that my life has been a love
letter to the church.

Age 14

Dear Church,

*I finally feel like I'm a part of a family again. I would be so lonely
without you. I don't even have to do anything except show up. I
didn't even know that the leaders knew my name, but I got a card
in the mail today saying, "Janell! Come back for youth group next
week!" Things are pretty miserable at home and I'm thankful to
have an escape. I would be totally lost without you. To be honest,
sometimes I feel lost during "big church" too, but all my friends and
I sit in the same pews each week and everyone knows that we are
the YOUTH GROUP, so at least I feel connected.*

XoXo,
Janell

Age 15

Dear Church,

I really love you. I got baptized today and so many people were there. I'm so excited. I think this is the best day of my life. On top of that, I do my quiet times almost every morning like you told me to and I threw away my Student Bible because I understand that the King James Version is where it's at. I'm really sorry about the mis-understanding.

Since I am a legitimate member now, I'm going to work so hard to prove that I belong. I'm committed to bringing my friends here with me and I'm already praying about who I can bring to summer camp. Also, I think our accountability group is going to be, like, really awesome this year. You won't regret letting me in. I'm going to be so good at this. You'll see.

All my heart,
Janell

MISSION

Forsake Your
Purified Space

Kester Brewin

To the Church of North America,

To those across the water, to my dear brothers and sisters in Christ, a vast ocean separates us. Some of you there left these shores some four hundred years ago, and sailed across that vast and dangerous sea to settle in a new and wonderful land. We hadn't pushed the Reformation far enough, so you left us, navigated a watery wilderness for weeks on end, a sea in which the waves did not miraculously part to speed your safe passage, you risked all in order to find your paradise. You left to build utopia, and this, my dear brothers and sisters, is what I think the Lord is saying in all of North America now: you must abandon your pursuit of paradise if you are ever to see the kingdom of heaven.

• • •

Utopia is a dangerous ideal. Obsessed with the sinfulness and fallenness of the world, a new place is colonized and ground is burned and cleared. A community withdraws to a purified space to build the New World, which, rooted in the Word of God, will be perfect and eternal.

All conflict will be eliminated by this reordering of society. Or at least that is the hope. But, as Anthony Dworkin notes, these utopian communities "cannot fulfill their objectives without attempting to remake *human nature*, and can't remain utopian without fighting to eliminate groups within society that are seen as agents of corruption."[1]

Because utopia is created as a pure space, utopia demands violence to fight for the continued purity of this space. Walls are built to keep corruption out. Boundaries are formed, which must be defended.

But attack can be the best form of defense. Rather than fighting to keep our own space pure, why not take up arms, march out and fight to purify more land? Axes of evil that threaten us by their impurity should be taken in hand and cleansed.

Witches should be burned in Salem. Communists rooted out. Suspicious people should be rounded up and questioned at length. Mosques should not be built, and presidents should be whiter than white and have a totally unimpeachable birthright. Foreign companies should be blamed, and the Inuit relocated. Homosexuals should be silenced, and though social networks should be embraced and friendship counts worshiped, those who begin to talk of socialism should have their tongues surgically removed by well-oiled private healthcare firms.

Explorers discovered a newfound land, Puritans left England to make . . . New England, withdrawing from the world in order to create a dreamland, both purging the places they found in order to create utopia.

But you must abandon your pursuit of paradise, if you are ever to see the kingdom of heaven. For your Savior was never a Puritan. Conceived outside of marriage, born into an animal's bed, visited by outcast shepherds, worshiped by foreign astrologers, cast out into foreign lands, brought up under occupation, rejected by his family—here was a man who knew what God required. This dirty-handed deity reached out to lepers, ate with pariahs, was anointed by prostitutes, spoke openly with women, caused chaos in the temple and saved his harshest words for those who would paint their sepulchers white.

Your freedom, your salvation, was won by a man branded a dirty heretic, a man condemned with criminals, a man strung up on a tree as one who had even been condemned by God.

The sheet comes down from heaven and God says kill and eat, and you say "but Lord . . ." and protest your longstanding cleanliness while God interrupts and demands that you do not brand as dirty that which God has deemed pure. "I now realize how true it is that God does not show favoritism but accepts those from *every* nation who fear him and do what is right" (Acts 10:34-35 TNIV, emphasis added).

My dear brothers and sisters, you have done so much that is right. Toronto was a blessing; America, the land of the free, with your statutes of liberty and high principles of justice. All of you have fought the good fight and sided with the just and worked hard. And God knows that, in you, the pure in heart are blessed. But hear this: no one is free until everyone is free; no one will enter heaven unless their hands are dirty.

So even as the times become tougher, do not turn away from the other. Do not turn away from the poor, from the marginalized, from minorities, from Muslims, from Palestinians, from gays, from the elderly, from the homeless. Do not turn away from the misunderstood, from the hurting, from the fearful.

The "other" has a face, and it is a book in which good is written. You ask, How can I enter the kingdom of God? The answer is as it always has been: Love. Bloody, painful, aching, weeping, water-transforming, bread-multiplying, tax-collector-melting love. Love them even if they hurt you. Love them even if they hate you and trump up charges against you and string you up and kill you. And if they do, then remember these words and repeat them: "Forgive them Father, for they do not know what they are doing." Your Father knows what you are doing. He sees all, knows all. Sees the new puritans holding their tea parties and hears the cries of hatred from those who are wounded.

The book of revenge is now closed. This is a new testament, a new covenant, with a new spirit whose fruit is pure, sweet and complex love. Love for neighbors. Love for the noisy person next door. Love for the addicts down the street. Love for the bored teenagers on the corners. Love for those of a different color. Love for those with different views. Love for those who seek power. Love for those obsessed with money. Love for those who flame you online. Love for those who need support. Love for those who don't bless North America.

This is the love that drove God from heaven and into the body of a tiny Palestinian child. This is the love that stripped him of power, of knowledge, of glory, of security, of adoration and reduced him to reliance on a poor mother's milk in a filthy cave.

Abandon your purified, sterile churches. Nothing can live in a sterilized environment. Come join God in the dirt. You are God's friends if you do what God commands: love one another, in the same way that God has loved you.

Amen, and amen.

On No Longer
Counting the Cost

Sarah Lance

Dear Beloved,

I bring with me greetings from my friends in Kolkata, the women of Sari Bari, a business of hope, creating opportunities for freedom for women trapped in the sex trade, and also from the women of Sonagacchi, our many friends who remain bonded in the sex trade, for whose freedom we continue to hope. These are heroic women of strength and wisdom, are the mentors of faith that guide my language, my heart and my burden for the body of Christ.

I have forgotten much of who I knew God to be before I met these women, learned their stories and walked with them in times of deep suffering and of great joy. They have taught us what is truly valuable.

The women of Sonagacchi, most of whom remain trapped in the dark lanes of Kolkata's infamous red light district, have taught us how to mourn. This year the loss of our friend Pornima was devastating for us, and in the midst of that loss as community we found what it means to be comforted when we mourn and we found the beauty of community and God's pres-

ence as we welcomed one another's tears and offered and received healing embraces.

Bharoti and Minu have given me eyes to see that the impossible becomes possible with faith. Bharoti, who comes out of
the most horrific circumstances, is a light of hope—a mother
and missionary for girls who remain trapped in the sex trade.
Minu prays and God answers; the fruit of her prayers opens
doors for more girls and women to have freedom.

Arotun, Aroti and Tinki have helped me understand the importance of celebration and laughter. These moments of celebration bringing both healing and release. At Sari Bari we
celebrate with food and dance, marking the beautiful moments
of our shared life together.

Jillik and Rina have taught me about friendship, generosity
and interruptibility. It is a gift to share life with these women
who give so completely of themselves and serve those around
them with such abandon.

All of the women have taught me about compassion and the
importance of suffering with those who hurt. The women at
Sari Bari have been deeply wounded and in some cases continue to find themselves in places of abuse, yet they show deep
compassion for their sisters who remain in the sex trade, for
those of us who struggle to support them and for the men who
have offended them.

The women at Sari Bari are beautiful treasures, holding
within them pearls of great price. Every single one of them is
taking heroic steps toward freedom and new life. They embody
restoration and transformation in one of the most impossible
places to live in the world. These women have given the words
to my heart for this letter. They have taught me there is no
cause powerful enough to compel me to stay in Kolkata; there
are only relationships, and these women and their families are

my anchor. There is no gain in counting the cost, looking back to what I might have given up, because the treasures of heaven are at my disposal in the presence of a God who has given more than I could ask or imagine.

Yes, God gave us in Kolkata a dream for the freedom of women trapped in the sex trade, and yet it is only a small part of the larger dream to restore humanity. God gave us, a part of the body of Christ, a dream for the world. A dream of the lost being found, of ruins being restored and of the darkness being exposed to the light. We have held that dream, literally. We have held God's heart in our hands, felt it beating and were compelled to press it to our own chests, letting its unbearable burden of love mark us, change us, refuse to allow us to take our own paths.

God has given us a dream larger than one person, one denomination or one people group could possibly make a reality. We are a part of the dream for the whole body, for the whole of humanity. We are compelled to keep dreaming for things we may never see. Believing in *hope* for a reality that we may never witness. Believing with faith that the impossible will become possible. As the hands that extend from the body holding the beating heart of God for the world, we can bring hope to the hopeless, bread to the hungry, forgiveness to the oppressor, freedom for the enslaved and family to the lonely. As God's body, we let that beating heart mark those with whom we have a relationship.

We know the marks of God's love for the world are made apparent in the sacrifice of Jesus, the willingness of the Son of God to suffer personal and sacrificial loss, the act of touching and healing the afflicted and befriending the least, embracing and being embraced in human community, and the willingness to be obedient even in the face of being maligned and killed.

These marks of God's love have touched us, but we have struggled to allow them to transform our lives. We so often desire a plan, five steps to a rich, passionate life of love, to vocation, to certainty of future purpose. Yet the God of the universe does not work with a five-step plan or even a five-year plan. The plan extends for generations—a plan to bring about transformation in the minutes, days, years and hundreds of years, to raise up the age-old foundations and restore us to the garden.

We have been given the opportunity to feel God's heart for the world, to experience the beauty of God's image reflected in the faces of our neighbors, to have not only our minds but our actions, our use of language and our experience of the world transformed. This has made us passionate advocates of great causes but loving the cause is not enough.

God is more interested in the hearts of people than cause-oriented propaganda. So many of us are satisfied with a cause. The cause is our passion, but the people of the cause are lost. They have become stories on our T-shirts that have no meaning. What are the names of the people in the cause for which you serve? Do you know their hearts, their stories and their language? We love the cause, yet so little penetrates our hearts and moves us to the radical love that requires real relationship with broken humans. Cause is incapable of moving us to change our lives, redirect our resources or release control of our futures. The God of love gave Christ for the people, not the cause. It is *people*, whose stories we know, whose hearts we love and whose burdens we share, that will bring about the transformation of so many broken realities and leave God's mark of love on the world.

Jesus knew the names of those he healed. He touched them and embraced and was embraced by them. The Christ came to the most devastated, and aligned himself in such a way that he was maligned and called a drunkard. If we are not being maligned, scandalizing those who still sleep in the church, then we are missing the incarnational call to love the world's most vulnerable, the world's exiled, the world's most wounded. Our concern should be what the poor and prostituted think of us, what the God of the universe thinks of us, not what those around us think of us.

We must reject the culture of personality and embrace the people around us. Loving them, giving our lives for them. We cannot look at what we will receive or to count the cost or look around for who might notice what we are doing. Remember, we have God's heart; we have held it in our hands, felt it beating, and we know, we must know, we are beloved. We must be the beloved for the beloved—regardless of cost.

It has been said that we North Americans know the cost of everything and the value of nothing.[2] We spend days, months, years keeping an accounting of all that we have given up for our faith. We await the repayment and miss the returns on our investment. All the time and energy we have spent for the kingdom is accounted for and awaits repayment in the form of an unanswered wish list of personal desires. It is a fruitless and defeating endeavor to continue counting the cost. If we are only counting the cost, we will misunderstand what is of true value and the means by which we will receive the most profound returns.

If we continue counting the cost, we will only know what everything costs. We will not understand the value of what we are able to receive when cost does not matter.

Pearls of great price have been hidden for us in the forgotten places among the forgotten people of the world. To find the kingdom of God among the poor, to receive comfort as we wait with those who mourn, to know the meaning of peacemaking in places where the battle to survive is minute by minute. Will we not give all that we have to posses these treasures?

We must allow ourselves to be rescued by those who live in poverty, by those who suffer. Let them teach us about the heart of God. We believe we have everything, but we so often lack the very things that are most valuable. Things that can be learned in companionship with those who suffer and mourn and yet celebrate with abandoned joy, those who find community and family in the most unlikely places.

Some may travel to the ends of the earth to make their homes in slums and red-light areas, yet we only need to have the eyes to see the Kolkatas in our own contexts.

We are not saviors but tools. We are the God-stamped instruments of love in the world. We are simply the rough machinery of the kingdom, hands and feet of a Master who desires to use us—our brokenness, our stories, our pains—for the redemption and glory of a maligned Savior.

Beloved, we must let God's love move us into relationship with people who live in poverty, with both the victims and the offenders; we must give our lives for the people God loves. Feeding the slaughtered sheep. Sitting with the needy in the ash heaps, awaiting their triumphal rescue. Being among those who have so little, letting their generosity and friendship teach us. We need to forget what it might cost and remember the value of all that God will do whether we see it with our own eyes or not.

Many before us did not see the fruit of their labors and yet they labored anyway, believing with faith that God heard them and would fulfill his promises. Having not seen, having not counted the cost, they moved forward into God's purposes, trusting that they were meant to be a part of the plan, a part of

God's eternal plan. They did not seek fame or wear T-shirts that spoke of the credit they deserved for the actions they took on behalf of the kingdom. They lived with the difficulty of yet-unanswered prayers, holding—sometimes desperately—to faith, embracing God and being marked by perfect love. They died before they saw the fulfillment of the promise, yet we know the promises were kept.

Are we afraid to let God take our hearts and stamp his love on them. Let us take our hearts from our chests, forgetting the cost, and offer them to the beloved who line the lanes of the red-light areas, women we can call by name; the beloved who will die in hunger, whose mother could be our friend; the children and youth on the street, whose stories we desire to know intimately, who will be arrested today with no advocate or defender. Let us offer them our hearts. Let us receive vocation in fragments built out of friendships and partnerships with those who reflect Jesus and mark the reality of the present kingdom! As we wait with our friends for restoration and redemption, we will find the things of greatest value—community with those who suffer at the center, friendship, generosity, beauty and our own poverty that will lead us to interdependence and submission.

Beloved body, my prayer for us is that we will dream for things we may never see. Believing with faith that the impossible will become possible for those who know no possibility. May our lives be changed by the story of one person. May they be transformed by the stories of ten people whom we call friends. May these stories destroy us, may they give us hope, may they bring about healing and restoration both to the hearer and the speaker. Let us seek out the treasures of heaven in the forgotten places, not counting the cost but welcoming the gifts that God gives in relationship with those to

whom the kingdom has been promised. Let our prayers go up
to the heavens with the names of our friends on our lips, let
our pleas for justice and restoration for God's beloved over-
whelm the heavens!

Oh great God, have mercy on us.

The Ideologizing
of the Church

David Fitch

To all the Christians in North America,

The North American church is in a credibility crisis. We find ourselves in a culture that no longer sees Christianity to be true, relevant, or, for that matter, interesting. Yet we keep doing church the same way—as if nothing has changed. We continue to do Sunday morning (and Sunday evening) services, put on Christian rock concerts, do outreach events and hang out in the fellowship hall. We do it all seeking to reach the world with the gospel, but we discover that only Christians are showing up. Meanwhile our neighbors and our world go on oblivious to the good news of Jesus Christ. We are looking more and more like a people having a conversation with ourselves that no one else cares about.

We compete with each other on producing better Sunday morning services. This usually means excellent music, the best video technology or the most charismatic and easy to listen to Bible teacher. Yet we know, by and large, these kinds of services change little in our lives and communities. Few remember anything from the morning sermon. The so-called worship experience with its wonderful music and playful dramas serves to excite us but rarely affects us beyond the moment. Instead the "show" seems to distract us from noticing the ways our lives don't make sense as followers of Christ. Yet we keep on doing it because it reinforces us in thinking that we are doing something significant.

We keep counting what we call "decisions for Christ" in our churches. Yet we know most of these decisions don't mean anything. Statistics continue to show that only a small percentage of our recorded "decisions" are made by people who will still be following Jesus a year later. And yet, like the teenager who keeps going forward in the Baptist church service week after week, "making sure" of his decision one more time, we keep doing this. We intuitively know this ritual is making no connection to the way people live, but we can't stop ourselves.

The progressives among us do the same thing with justice. We create enormous energy around justice issues in the name of God. Some impressive money is raised and some good works are done in the name of Jesus. But often, too often I suggest, the word *justice* becomes a bumper-sticker-like rallying cry that makes us feel better rather than accomplishing anything that actually takes root in our lives. Sadly, we participate very little in actual relationships with the poor that live alongside us in our churches or near our church buildings. It is much like buying fair trade coffee at Walmart. Nonetheless we keep doing it.

When someone keeps doing the same things year after year even when the reason for doing them is gone, we say they have lost their sanity. The grieving husband who keeps bringing coffee to his wife years after she has died, and the shell-shocked soldier who keeps asking if the war is over years after his discharge, have lost touch with the reality they are living. Like them, the church keeps doing the same things we did fifty years ago even though it has little or no connection to our everyday lives. In many parts of the country where Christendom is all but gone, we are conducting church as if we are insane.

And so, in this time of insanity, we need to take a look at ourselves.

I contend that one of the best ways to understand what we're doing is to study ourselves as an ideology. Ideology has been called "false consciousness" because it can keep us doing the same behaviors over and over again while covering over the contradictions that would make us question what we're doing. By studying ideology, we can help people see the contradictions. When it becomes apparent we are saying one thing while doing something quite the opposite, the emptiness in our way of life is revealed. We end up manufacturing justifications and even enemies to keep the church going. Contradictions appear. Lies get revealed. Our ideology loses its credibility and it goes into a crisis.

There are reasons to suspect that this is what is happening among us as the church in North America. For instance, sadly, over the past twenty years we have become known more in North America for our duplicity, judgmentalism and dispassion than the gospel. Whether it is because of "the evangelical right" and the various *New York Times* bestseller "hate books" written toward it, or the megachurch pastors that get caught in sex scandals, evangelical Christians are now a people who are best known for our fighting against gay people, fighting against those who don't believe in absolute truth (read as "those who don't believe like we do") or the liberal political agenda. We are living in contradiction to the gospel. Whatever is to blame, our way of life as evangelicals has failed to make the gospel compelling in the society we find ourselves in. We're looking very much like an ideology that is losing its credibility and is in crisis.

This process of ideologization does not happen overnight. It

kind of sneaks up on us. What started out as a gathering of
people around something very real gets compromised over
time. There are new situations that challenge the status quo.
Perhaps there is a grasping for power that seeps in and wants to
use the gathering. Change is needed. Yet, over time, instead of
changing our behavior, we develop reasons to keep things
going. Our beliefs, together with the way we practice them, become an ideology that effectively works to keep the majority
comfortable and certain people in power. Soon we lose touch
with the reality that brought us together in the first place.

Is this what has happened to North American Christians?

When an ideology is in crisis, its leaders get defensive. We
find enemies to rally people against in an effort to keep the system going. Unfortunately, the church in North America is now
defined more by what we are against than who we are or what
we are for. This kind of ideology happens all the time in our
churches. We notice it when someone says "Oh that church is
the *Bible-preaching church*—they believe in the Bible," implying
the others don't. Or "We're the church that believes in *community*." The others somehow don't. "That church? They're the *gay
church* and that one is the church that is *anti-gay*. We're the
church that plants gardens and loves the environment," and
"Oh, by the way you're the church of the SUVs." On and on it
goes as our churches get identified by what we are against. We
get caught up in perverse enjoyments like "I am glad we're not
them!" or "See, I told you we were right!" In the process we get
distracted from the fact that things haven't really changed at all,
that our lives are caught up in gamesmanship, not the work of
God's salvation in our own lives and his work (*missio Dei*) to
save the world. This cycle of ideologization works against the
church. It is short-lived and it breeds an antagonistic relation to
the world. In the process we become a hostile people incapable

of being the church of Jesus Christ in mission.

And so today, this week and in the months that lie ahead, we must join together as Christians to break this cycle of ideological church. I suggest we can do this by "going local." We can resist the ideologizing of the church by refocusing our attention on our local contexts. In going local, we inherently refuse to organize around what we are against and instead intentionally gather to participate in God's mission in our neighborhoods, our streets, among the peoples that we live our daily lives with. Here we gather not around ideas extracted from actual practice in life that we then turn into ideological banners, but around the participation in the bounteous new life God has given us in Jesus Christ and his mission. We participate in his reign, the kingdom, by actually practicing the reconciliation, new creation, justice and righteousness God is doing and made possible in Jesus Christ. Here we become a people of the gospel again. It is only by doing this that God breaks the cycle of ideological church.

Christ has already given to us many practices by which his life is birthed in us in an actual time and place. To name a few, Christ and his apostles have taught us how to *inhabit place humbly*, listening, eating with, inhabiting and bringing peace (Luke 10:1-16). He (and his apostles) has taught us how to practice *reconciliation in conflict and discernment* (Matthew 18:15-20), participate in the *eucharistic* meal (Matthew 26:26-29; 1 Corinthians 11:17-33), *proclaim the good news* in a place (Luke 4), minister to the poor and broken (Matthew 25:34-46), share fellowship in the *gifts of the Spirit* (Ephesians 4), shape a new economics together (1 Corinthians 11:1-22; Acts 2:44-45). These are sacraments of place. They are sacraments because Christ extends his presence into the world through them in us, through us and into the world. Christ extends his reign into each new situation. The gospel is proclaimed situationally. We cannot ideologize this. We can only discern and cooperate with him and move forward in the mission. As we do these practices, we participate "in Christ" in the new world coming. We become birthed into a local expression of the kingdom of God in concrete life. The apostle Paul calls this form of communal politic *"the fullness of Christ"* (Ephesians 4:13), where such a plentitude of love and reconciliation is birthed that it bleeds seamlessly into the whole world.

As we look at the church in North America, it appears that the world can no longer make sense of what we assert to be true by looking at our lives. This is the crisis in our way of life, which is another way of saying "this is our ideological crisis." In these urgent days, therefore, let us stop everything and figure out what has gone wrong in the disparity between what we say and how we live. Let us return to the basic practices of being his people together in the places where we live. Let us pay attention to the Eucharist and the daily reconciliation we must practice in life with one another in this place. By reading and hearing the Word, let us pay attention to what God is saying and calling us into in our neighborhoods and responding with simple obedience. Let us pay attention to conflict and disagreements and see them as times to submit to one another in fear and trembling, seeking God's voice. It is out of these times that we shall see more clearly what we must do to cooperate with God's work in the world for his salvation. Let us minister and proclaim the gospel to the poor, to those who can teach us how to receive the gospel for our whole lives. Let us minister the gifts of the Spirit to each other, seeking the renewal of all things in our lives and in our neighborhoods. Let us seek the good of the city through the proclamation of the reign of Jesus Christ as Lord. And in so doing, the gospel shall take root in us and our neighborhoods. The ideologization of the church shall be resisted, and God in Christ shall take on flesh in us and come humbly into the neighborhood.

This push toward place is already happening all over North America. Amid all the noise and busyness of North American life, it is the manifesto of the gospel anew. Will we all join in? I see it already happening. Praise be to God.

An Unanxious Presence

Walter Brueggemann

To the Beloved Church Gathered Around
Our Lord Jesus in the United States,

We Christians live amid "the American Dream," which has defining power for all of us. That dream, from the outset, has had
enormous force and has always been linked to our evangelical
faith. Since the arrival of the Pilgrims—and then the Puritans—the dream of freedom of every sort has been allied with
the gospel, so much so that the American Dream and the Christian gospel have come to seem synonymous, and never more so
than now.

But something decisive has happened to the American
Dream. Either it has had, since the beginning, a down side of
greed-to-the-edge-of-violence, or it has morphed into something other than it was. In the last century the American Dream
has been transposed into an unbridled pursuit of power as empire and into an insatiable hunger for more commodities in
pursuit of an extravagant "good life." The several mantras of
"White Man's Burden," Manifest Destiny," "Leader of the Free
World" and "Democratic Capitalism" have become the trigger
terms to justify an irresponsible standard of self-indulgent liv-

ing and the rationale for the pursuit of more markets and more natural resources around the world, all of which seem to commit us to perpetual war. The outcome is a projection of hubris, arrogance and self-serving power that is, on the face of it, contradictory to a gospel way of life.

In these days of self-reflection, I suggest that the church has as a primary task the sorting out of the interface between American Dream (as it now is) and a gospel way of life that moves in quite different directions. This task of sorting out is not easy and cannot be obvious, because gospel faith has provided much of the energy and passion for our society. Because the task is neither obvious nor easy, it is important that the church address this issue thoughtfully, carefully, and in self-critical ways, without easy ideological formulas of rejection or affirmation. The interface of faith and culture in our society is complex and tricky, and admits of no simplistic resolution.

I suggest that the task before the church in this regard is three-fold. First, it is a task of the church to be *truth-telling* about the toxic aspects of our society that are, in sum, antineighborly in terms of greed that is powered by anxiety about the changing world. When the church—or parts of it—is implicated in a narrow and selfish individualism, the fabric of a viable society frays and eventually evaporates. The rich heritage of multicultural welcome is a defining dimension of our national heritage that must be prized, for the gospel—even "beforehand"—has been for "all the families of the earth" (Genesis 12:3 ESV; Galatians 3:8).

Second, it is the task of the church to think through and live out an *alternative* conduct and policy that exhibit its own passionate commitment to the gospel of love of God and love of neighbor. For starters, I suggest three dimensions of obedience that may be defining for a community with a gospel-shaped intention:

- Such an obedient church is mandated to practice *hospitality* based in the God who welcomes strangers.

- Such an obedient church is mandated to practice *generosity* that is based on the limitless generosity of the Creator God.

- Such an obedient church is mandated to *forgive*, to forgive as we have been forgiven.

These are perhaps the oldest disciplines of the church and, I believe, are now the most urgent and most contemporary. It is clear, moreover, that these three practices are deeply in contradiction to the dominant values of our society that are now constituted by a distorted notion of the American Dream:

- a society that is inhospitable to "others" unlike us

- a society that is increasingly parsimonious toward the neighbor

- a society that operates quid pro quo without the grace of forgiveness that breaks the vicious cycles of resentment and vengeance

Third, the church is not only called to be about alternative obedience in its own life (which it does more or less intuitively), but is called as well to the work of *reshaping public attitudes, public practices and public policies* in the same direction of justice, so that the social power of our society (in its political and economic forms) may be marked by hospitality, generosity and forgiveness. These elements of gospel obedience are, of course, set deeply into the fabric of our national identity, but have been crowded away or submerged by an ideology of antineighborliness that is grounded in anxiety acted out as greed.

It is my conviction that the "acting out" of the dominant script in our society is grounded in a profound anxiety that pervades our society. It is an anxiety about not being in control, not having enough, not being safe, not having things as they

were. As the world changes toward becoming "one world," we
Americans have it less and less on our own terms. Such anxiety,
fed by ideologues, is readily transformed into greed, anger, hate
and violence. This is a milieu, I believe, in which the church is
to live its life as much as possible outside that pervasive anxiety
that is destructive of the core values given in the American heritage that is grounded in the Bible.

I suggest, beloved Church, that the alternative to such anxiety—that is everywhere around us and that sweeps all before
it—is found in the keeping of sabbath rest. That possibility, of
course, stands at the center of the Ten Commandments and
anticipates a visible, intentional, regular discipline that leaves
us free and unencumbered in the face of the rat race of produc-
tion and consumption. Thus the "mandate to difference" is that
the church may refuse to participate in the anxiety of our society and so offer itself as "an unanxious presence" grounded in
God's limitless goodness. The church has, in many ways, been
seduced by the anxiety-grounded ideology of our society. A return to the simple truth of the gospel and the simple practice of
neighborliness will be profoundly subversive in our society and
wildly generative of well-being and joy.

The crisis in the German church under National Socialism
was that many church people wanted to have it both ways.
They did not want to choose between Hitler and the God of the
gospel, and saw no need to make such a decision. They imagined that the claims of the gospel and the hopes of National
Socialism were readily compatible. The phrase for such a refusal to choose and so to remain "lukewarm" was "cheap grace"
(Revelation 3:16). Mutatis mutandis, I submit that the same
seduction of "cheap grace" is among us, a refusal to choose
between the toxic forms of the American Dream so evident
among us and the gracious truthfulness of the gospel. A "harder

grace," filled with truth, is offered to us. It is an important task now in the church, I propose, to face this hard matter and in the process to find ourselves resituated in gracious goodness and much joy.

I write to you in the joy and hope of the gospel, myself facing the same decisions to which all of us are now summoned.

Interlude

Janell Anema (Age 16)

Dear Church,

Do you want to know a secret? I don't actually think I'm good at this. I don't know how to listen when I pray, except to the sound of my own anxious breaths. I don't even know how to sit alone with my thoughts, and with Jesus, and feel comfortable. I mostly feel insecure and inadequate—like I'm doing it wrong. I accepted Jesus into my heart when I was four (and then again every time anyone prayed the sinner's prayer, just to make sure it counted). I have hardly missed a Sunday service, but I still feel like a new Christian. I wish that you would help me with this. I am doing everything you keep telling me to do.

Don't tell anyone though. I'm probably the only one who feels like this and I'm really sorry I'm not doing it right. Just please don't tell.

Shhhhhhhh,
Janell

Dear Church

Today I didn't even listen to the message. Instead I sat in the back row and prayed for Pastor as he was teaching. I found myself hold-

ing my breath as I prayed that no one would cough and that no phone would ring because those are clearly tactics of the enemy to disturb the message. I prayed that no one would distract what God might be trying to communicate through Pastor. We are so lucky to have Pastor. He is so smart and charismatic and knows everything about how to make us the best church.

Yours in Service,
Janell

Church,

Why are you fighting? I haven't seen this much brokenness since my family fell apart. First, my mom asked my dad to move out, then the elders made Pastor leave and now the congregation is fighting, falling apart, breaking up. I thought you hated divorce.

Pastor committed a moral failure, and so he had to leave. Word must have gotten out about the affair, because people were hanging from the rafters the day Pastor was forced to resign. I never understood why funerals were held in churches until today. Now that attendance is back down, and the financial reports look bleak, some of your leaders are saying that Pastor should come back.

I don't get it. You convinced me that the Christian life is lived in black and white, that there is always wrong and right, and that God demands we live in the white, that we live in the light. So were you wrong then, or are you wrong now?
I'm confused. And scared.

Janell
P.S. I didn't think you could be wrong.

TRUTH

The Gospel
of the Bible

Tim Challies

Dear Church,

I love you. I'm proud to be part of you. I look around at all the
church is accomplishing in the world, all the ways it is living
out its mandate, and my heart is just full of joy, full of pride. I
see what so many of you are doing, how you are living, and I
want to let the whole world know, yes, I'm on their team! They're
on mine!

But Church, I've been asked to write you a letter. And in this
letter I want to challenge you on one thing, one fundamental
thing that seems like it may be in danger of getting lost or getting kicked aside. In the middle of all we do, we may just be
losing sight of the heart of it all.

Church—the Bible tells us we are brothers and sisters—
we've got to get the gospel right. The true gospel. The real gospel. The gospel of the Bible, the one that stands at the very heart
of the Christian faith, the one on which the church stands or
falls. There are all kinds of gospels floating around out there,
all kinds of gospels competing with one another. And amid all
of these gospels, we need to discover, or rediscover, or cling to
and proclaim the real one, the true one, the only one that fully

and finally matters. The only one that saves. We have got to get the gospel right.

I want the church to be excited about new kinds of church community. But not unless we've got the gospel right. I want the church to be serving the poor, to be standing with the widow and orphan, to be living in a radically different way. But how can we really serve anyone else until we've got this one thing right?

So what is the gospel? What is this good news that gets Christians so excited? What does the Bible call us to believe, to embrace, to take into all the world? That's what I want to share with you now.

If you haven't heard the gospel message before, then listen in and hear how this is good news. If you've heard the gospel message a million times, then listen in again and let it thrill you. It's not just good news; it's the best news. It can thrill the heart again and again and again. It just never gets old, we never master it, we never grow beyond it. The gospel is what saves us, the gospel is what motivates us, the gospel is what sustains us.

The gospel is about God. It's about humanity. It's about Christ. And it's about you and me—about our response, our action, our obedience.

The gospel starts with God. It has to since God is the Creator, the one who conceived of this world and who brought it into existence. He made me and he made you. And what is this God like? He is holy, he is kind, he is loving, and he is utterly perfect in every way. There is no fault in God, no sin, no weakness, no injustice, no lack of perfection. We love all this about God. These are the qualities we like best.

God is also just. This may be one of those character qualities we are guilty of losing sight of, this idea that God is just, that he will never let guilt go unpunished, that he *can* never let sin go unpunished. It isn't in his character to do so.

And so the gospel is about God because it starts with God; everything starts with God. It's about this God who created the world and who rules over it, who loves it and cares for it.

But it's also about humans. God created us in his image, creatures who bear the mark of the Creator. We were made in his image and told to imitate him, to obey him, to fulfill his command that we act as his agents in his world. In all things we are to magnify him, to bring glory to him—the glory he deserves. He gave us all we needed to do this, all we needed to perfectly obey his every wish, his every command.

But we rebelled. We sinned. We put ourselves in the place of God, we sought to have all of the benefits of God without actually having relationship with him. We committed an act of cosmic treason, putting ourselves in the place of the one who made us. All of us have sinned, and all of us fall short of the glory of God, the perfection God demands of us. None of us are righteous. Not one. And so we enter into this story, into this gospel, as people who are at odds with God, people who have deliberately forsaken the one who created us. This has made us not just sinners, not just people who sin, but people who are captivated by sin, enslaved by it, who love it. We are slaves to sin.

This ought to bother us. It ought to grieve us. It also ought to terrify us. In rejecting God, we have called down upon ourselves his judgment. We have invited him to exercise his justice, the justice that sin demands. Actually, we've demanded it! The wages of sin is death; the proper repayment, the proper reward for sin, is death. This is a physical death and a spiritual death—a death of the body and the inevitable consequence that a soul will be judged, it will be punished forever. If there is anything unpopular in the church today, it is this notion that hell exists, that it is a real place and that it is the final place for those who remain in rebellion against God. But this is exactly what the Bible tells us. It warns us that if we remain in our sin, if we remain enemies of God, we will be punished there for all eternity. We will face the furious wrath of a God who must see that justice is done.

We call the gospel "good news," but so far it sounds like a whole lot of bad news. It sounds like the worst news imaginable. We are sinful people who have invited an eternity of punishment upon ourselves. Where's the good in that?

Well, that's the beauty of the gospel. The full beauty and clarity of a diamond can only be seen against the black backdrop. And the beauty and goodness of the gospel can only be appreciated against that same dark backdrop of sin and death and judgment. The gospel is mercy, but only if we see it in the context of justice.

The gospel is about God, the perfect Creator; it is about humans, unrighteous sinners. But the gospel does not end here. Thank God for that. The gospel is also about Jesus Christ.

Here is God the just, the Creator, who made all that exists, the perfect and holy God. And here are humans, who were made holy but who chose to rebel, who chose to commit treason against the King of the universe. For God to be brought back into relationship with us, it would take a Mediator, it would take someone who could bridge the gulf between humans and God. It would take a man who is God.

Two thousand years ago a man named Jesus was born in a little town called Bethlehem. Born of a virgin, he was born entirely free of sin. Born of a woman, he was a son of men; conceived by God, he was the son of God. He was God incarnate, God incarnated in a human body, the Creator in the body of something he created. For a little over thirty years he lived on this earth totally and entirely free from sin. He obeyed God in every thought, in every deed, in every motive of his heart. In all things, even the smallest thought, the dreams in the middle of the night, the whispered words, the reaction to being sinned against, he loved God with all of his heart and his neighbor as himself. Never once did he slip up. Never once did he sin.

Jesus proclaimed that he was the Messiah, the long-awaited Savior, the one who could mediate the relationship of humans to God and God to humans, the one who could bring them back together. And how the people hated him. They mocked him. They followed him when the going was good and deserted him when the going was tough. They hung on his every word one day and screamed at him to shut his mouth the next. And still he loved them; still he honored God at every moment.

When the people could take it no more, they demanded that he be killed, that he be slaughtered, that he face the death of a common criminal. And so the Son of God, who is God himself, who is the one who created all the world, was hung on a cross and left to die. The cross is a horrific way to die, one of the most barbaric inventions of the twisted human mind. But for Christ the suffering was even worse. While he was on that cross, God turned his back on his Son. For the first time in all of eternity, Jesus was cut off from his Father, cut off from all that is good and beautiful in the world. And on that cross Jesus took sin upon himself. He became sin, he took all the ugliness and bitterness and murder and rape and violence. And on that cross he was punished for this sin. Hanging there, with nails through his hands and feet, he faced the full and furious wrath of God against sin. Hanging there between heaven and earth, he was rejected by humans and rejected by God. On the cross it was as if all of creation turned to Christ and cried "God . . . damn . . . you."

But something remarkable happened there. Something truly miraculous. After hours of the punishment of hell, Jesus spoke.

"It is finished!" he cried. It is finished. The work was done. He had borne up under the wrath of God, he had suffered all he needed to suffer. He had done what he came to do. He had taken sin upon himself and had suffered the necessary judgment for it. And with that he gave up his spirit. His body died.

But death couldn't hold him. How could death rule over the Creator? The third day his body was raised. The third day he walked out of that tomb. He was alive! He was resurrected. He had conquered death. He had won.

But the gospel doesn't end there. The gospel is not just a story, not just facts or narrative or history. The gospel demands a response. It calls us to believe it, to live by it, to proclaim it.

The gospel calls us to believe it. We are to believe not just the facts of it, that God is holy, that we are sinners, that Christ is the Savior, the one who stands between God and us. Though certainly those are facts we do need to believe. But we are called to faith. We are called to put our faith in Jesus, in this perfect Savior. We are to trust in Christ, to rely on him, to find in him all we need to be reconciled to the Father. We are to trust in Christ alone through faith alone, relying on Jesus to save us. This faith is a verb, it is an action, it is something we do, not something we have. We trust in Jesus, day in and day out, in good times and bad, in life and in death.

And when we do this, when we trust in Christ, when we put our faith in him, something truly remarkable happens. Christ trades our sinfulness for his righteousness. Christ saves us from what we deserve. He renews us. He gives us new life. If only we believe, if only we trust.

We are to believe, and we are to repent. We are to turn from the ways we used to live, the ways we want to live, and we are to follow Christ. We are to learn how he calls us to live, and we are to honor him, obey him. We don't do this out of compulsion but out of joy, out of gratitude, out of thanksgiving, out of love.

And having believed, having repented, the gospel calls us to the act of proclamation. This news is far too good to keep to ourselves. This news takes us from death to life, from fear to confidence, from purposelessness to true meaning, true significance. How could we keep such a message to ourselves? What kind of hypocrisy would that be? What kind of selfishness?

No, we need to take this message into all the world, proclaiming it to all who will listen and even to those who won't. We need to take it to our friends and families, to our homes and churches, to our schools and offices. We need to preach it to one another, we need to preach it to ourselves. We need to believe it and live out of it. This is a message worth living for and it's a message worth dying for.

This is the gospel. This is the message that we need to understand, that we need to embrace, that we need to proclaim. If we get the gospel wrong, we've gotten our faith wrong. If we get the gospel wrong, we are wasting our time and everyone else's. This is the foundation we need to build on. This is the heart of the Christian faith.

And at the end of this letter I want to pause to ask, Have you believed this gospel? Have you believed this good news? Do you see God as the Creator, the one who made you to be in perfect, eternal, unblemished relationship with him? Do you see yourself as one who sins, one who even finds joy in sin? Do you see that you deserve to be punished by God for that sin? Do you see that his justice demands satisfaction?

Have you trusted in Christ? Have you put your faith in him, repenting of sin, turning away from it and turning toward God? I wouldn't want to close this letter without encouraging you to do that. Trust in Christ. Turn to him. Put your faith in him.

You have heard the gospel. God says that his Word never returns void. It always accomplishes something. You cannot hear news this good and be unaffected. This gospel will either soften your heart or it will harden it. Either it will draw you to the one who calls, to the one who offers peace, salvation. Or it will harden your heart as you reject the gospel, as you reject God himself. If you walk away with a hard heart, you remain under the curse of sin, under judgment. These gospel words will be used against you. They'll be used to condemn you, when you stand before the Lord.

Jesus Christ was cursed by God, punished for sin, put to death and brought to life so that he could give you this life, this eternal life, this life that will never end. Turn to him, believe him, trust in him.

And Church, get this gospel right. This gospel is good news; it is precious news; it is life-giving, soul-saving, heart-stirring. It is the power of God for salvation, it is the *only* means by which God calls people to himself. We simply can't lose sight of it. There's nothing better than it, nothing higher, nothing more exciting, nothing more to graduate to. We can't neglect it. We can't replace it with anything else. It is a difficult message to proclaim, but it's the message the world absolutely needs to hear.

If we preach a different message under the banner of the gospel, we call God's curse upon ourselves. The Bible tells us that we damn ourselves. God help us to faithfully proclaim this message.

Church—brothers and sisters—let's make sure that as we do all we do, we keep the good news central. Let's make sure that we've got the gospel right. For God's sake. For God's glory.

The Sin of Abstraction

Peter Rollins

To the Church in North America,

Grace and peace.

Such a short letter, designed as it is to address your vast and multifaceted body, is bound to commit a myriad of sins. And for this I must apologize in advance. But the limits of the task I was set and exigency of the times at hand compel me to throw caution to the wind and in a spirit of love write to you about a crisis I see unfolding at the present moment.

I shall not waste any time listing the failures that mark parts of your body, for they are well known to you already.

You already know that you should love your neighbor, that you should stand up for those who are forced to live on their knees, speak up for those without a voice and give willingly to the many who have nothing. And you are often very good at seeing the times when you fall short.

Overall, I must say that I see no lack of compassion in you. Indeed when you are confronted with those parts of your body who do not care for the poor, the rest of you is outraged. You rightly oppose those parts that have used their position in order to embezzle money, abuse people under their care, lie, steal, stand against social reforms and build kingdoms in their own name rather than in the name of love.

The lack of concern witnessed in the callous acts of the sickly parts are condemned as a clear failure to live into the new life testified to in the figure of Christ.

However, I am concerned that your obvious compassion can mask a much deeper and more insidious problem, a problem that may be described as the sin of *abstraction*.

The sin of abstraction refers to the act of blaming of an individual part without taking into consideration the wider context they were immersed in. To understand this we may reflect on how conflicts are presented in the news today. We are often saturated with images of war and various humanitarian efforts designed to bring an end to the destruction. More than this we are often presented with images of evil dictators and local heroes who put themselves into danger in order to save others.

These images appear concrete to us because they are actual reflections of what is currently taking place. However these so-called concrete images have been divorced from the political, social and religious background that enables us to understand the conflict. As such they are really abstract images. For they have been pulled out of the opaque background that would enable us to understand how the conflict arose, what sustains it and how to move beyond it.

In the same way there is a limitation to removing or reforming cancerous parts of the body. For, by doing this, we fail to see how the personification of the illness in a part of the body is itself a manifestation of a deeper illness within the body itself.

There are any number of political systems that are filled with corrupt individuals. Politicians who take bribes, offer favors to friends or seek their own betterment over and above the betterment of those under their care. In such situations a basic type of political reform involves expelling such individuals.

However, we must not make the mistake of thinking that a political system without corrupt individuals will lead to a just system. For there are political systems in which most of the people involved are compassionate, kind and considerate while societal injustice continues unchecked. The reason for this relates to the way that the corruption is no longer connected with an individual or party, but is integrated into the very working of the system itself. As such those involved in the system can be kind and compassionate while fully participating in injustice.

For example, we can imagine parents going into a supermarket and buying their child some chocolate as a treat. As they are doing this, they notice someone stealing from the same stand. They are rightly angered and tell a security guard who promptly arrests the shoplifter.

In this situation we witness the law-abiding parents and the criminal who breaks the law. The problem, however, is that we can fail to look at the situation in its wider context. For it is likely that the chocolate bar which the parents bought was made with cocoa beans picked from the Ivory Coast by children the same age as their own, children who have no rights, who work inhumane hours and who suffer continual abuse. Here we can say that while it is clear that there is a law and a crime that transgresses the law, we can miss the way in which the legal system itself, in its failure to question how the chocolate gets to the shops, is itself criminal. The point here is that the parents rightly can feel moral and just while wholly participating in an immoral and unjust system.

The question I wish to present for your consideration is this: What if you are in a similar position today?

What if the love you affirm and the fruits of the Spirit you seek to share in your daily life actually mask a deeper illness that encourages the very opposite of these fruits at a structural level? What if the problem is not fundamentally one of certain parts being corrupt, but rather of these parts being symptoms of a much deeper and more far-reaching corruption?

There was a time in the recent past when Christians of various stripes passionately demanded that we take good care of slaves. They proclaimed that they should be treated with respect, that they should be cared for and that they should not be abused.

It took others to point out the absurdity of this position. The point was not to show virtue and kindness to slaves but rather to demand a society in which slavery would be banished.

Today you give generously to those who are homeless, organizing gift days, flea market sales and clothing collections. But surely the point is not to treat the homeless with dignity but rather to help create a society within which homelessness is no longer a reality. Indeed, instead of making the situation better, giving some spare change can actually be destructive in the long term, as it can help you feel that you are doing something good when you are actually allowing a horrible injustice to continue.

By acting in this way you can come to resemble the man who, early one morning, turned up at the house of his minister in tears, saying, "Please, can you help. A kind and considerate family in the area is in great trouble. The husband recently lost his job, and the wife cannot work due to health problems. They have three young children to look after, and the man's mother lives with them because she is unwell and needs constant care. They have no money at the moment, and if they don't pay the rent by tomorrow morning the landlord is going to kick them all onto the street, even though it's the middle of winter." In response the minister replied, "That's terrible. Of course we will help, I will go get some money from the church fund to pay their rent. Anyway how do you know them?" To which the man replied, "Oh, I'm the landlord!"

Here the landlord is able to think that he is a part of the solution while actually being a part of the problem. In the same way, you can believe deeply in love, forgiveness and the betterment of society, even affirming these beliefs through weekly small group meetings, membership of organizations and prayer groups, without it being lived out. For what if your values are found not in what you espouse but rather in what pours out of you?

The problem can be expressed in the story of a man who crosses a border regularly with a wheelbarrow full of junk. The border guards eventually get a tip off that he is smuggling stuff over the border. So each time he passes their checkpoint, they stop him, search him and look through the old junk in the wheelbarrow but they never find anything of interest. Many years later, after he has stopped crossing the border, one of the guards sees him drinking in a bar and approaches saying, "Come on, we know you were smuggling something all those years; tell me, what was it?" In response the man turned to him and said, "Why, I was smuggling wheelbarrows of course!"

Instead of looking "within" in order to find out what you really believe, what if what you believe is hidden in your very material reality and in what it produces? We must remember that the "heart" in the biblical context does not relate to the inner life but rather to the individual in his or her being as a whole. Indeed, within the Gospels we find a potent example of this when Peter vigorously insists that he would never deny his Messiah. In the Gospel of Mark we read,

"You will all fall away," Jesus told them, "for it is written:

'I will strike the shepherd,
and the sheep will be scattered.'

But after I have risen, I will go ahead of you into Galilee." Peter declared, "Even if all fall away, I will not."

"I tell you the truth," Jesus answered, "today—yes, to-night—before the rooster crows twice you yourself will disown me three times."

But Peter insisted emphatically, "Even if I have to die with you, I will never disown you." And all the others said the same. (Mark 14:27-31)

Here Jesus brings Peter face-to-face with a truth about his life, yet Peter is unable to accept it—what Jesus says does not match up with the image he has of himself. Later we read,

While Peter was below in the courtyard, one of the servant girls of the high priest came by. When she saw Peter warming himself, she looked closely at him.

"You also were with that Nazarene, Jesus," she said.

But he denied it. "I don't know or understand what you're talking about," he said, and went out into the entryway.

When the servant girl saw him there, she said again to those standing around, "This fellow is one of them." Again he denied it.

After a little while, those standing near said to Peter, "Surely you are one of them, for you are a Galilean."

He began to call down curses on himself, and he swore to them, "I don't know this man you're talking about."

Immediately the rooster crowed the second time. Then Peter remembered the word Jesus had spoken to him: "Before the rooster crows twice you will disown me three times." And he broke down and wept. (Mark 14:66-72)

It is not enough for you to say that you are falling short of your beliefs, for this very confession plays into the idea that there is a difference between your various beliefs and your actions. Rather, if you will permit, I ask you to remember the radical Christian insight that one's actions reflect one's beliefs. That you cannot say that you believe in God if you do not commit yourself to what Kierkegaard referred to as the work love.

In Alcoholics Anonymous the first act in the journey of healing is taken when the individuals stop speaking lies to themselves about themselves and admit to the reality of their material situation. The individuals publicly tell others their name and admit what, up until then, they have been denying. Namely that they have a problem, that they are an alcoholic.

What would it take for you to stop in your tracks? To stop aiming your energy at reforming parts of your body and rather to see these parts as mere symptoms of a much wider problem? What would it take for you to acknowledge a more far-reaching disease? What would it take for you to move beyond your obsession with right belief and personal piety so as to become a force of real change in the world? What would it take . . . ?

The Fulcrum
and Linchpin

James Shelley

To the Church of North America,

Hear this: interpreting Scripture is the fulcrum and linchpin of your historical existence. Whether it's King Josiah discovering forgotten texts in the basement of the temple, Martin Luther making Scripture accessible to everyone or Ron Luce inducing thousands of teenagers to wail in repentance—every reformation, renewal and rebirth of the Christian faith pivots around the interpretation (and therefore the integration) of Scripture.

Your faith depends on your presuppositions about the Bible. The implications of this realization are all encompassing. Any statement that begins with, "The Bible says . . ." is actually a statement about what the *speaker* believes. This is equally true whether you are Rob Bell or John McArthur. You are all working from the same source material here. The chant of Joel Osteen, waving the Bible above his head and pledging allegiance to the words therein, is ultimately no different from an exegesis of Jesus' compassion by Shane Claiborne, in that both are rooted in individual interpretations and assumptions about what the

Bible is, generated by their prior presuppositions, ideals, experiences and convictions.

When you argue about Scripture, you are arguing your biases. If Mark Driscoll and Marcus Borg sat down to discuss their differences, underneath all the banter is nothing but two different presuppositions about the Bible. Who is "right" and who is "wrong" is ultimately a question of who has the "correct" interpretation about the Bible. But since both parties judge their own interpretations about the Bible by their own *presuppositions* of the Bible, both are ultimately appealing first and foremost to their own presuppositions. Dear Church, at some point you must recognize and name your camps and denominations for what they truly are: self-affirming cloisters of people who are happily comfortable with their self-validating presuppositions about Scripture.

Your next reformation comes when you abandon your arguments about what the Bible *says*, and invest your energy into investigating what the Bible *is*. Stop arguing about how to "apply the Word of God" and start formulating truly informed thoughts about church history, the nature of canon, and the doctrine of inspiration. Even if there were something concrete about these convictions explicit in the pages of Scripture itself, you would still have to account for your personal belief in those words. You must unearth and examine all these unchecked assumptions. You must delve deep into the matrix of your own assumptions about textual authority.

Herein will be the most painful and honest declaration of Christianity yet, for only when you seek to honestly address the beliefs you most desperately cherish can you genuinely declare your faith to be honest—honest to your own heart, mind and soul, and to God.

The Richness and Fullness of God's Image

Soong-Chan Rah

Dear Church,

This letter is written in the context of dramatic changes in Christianity in the early part of the twenty-first century. The center of gravity of the global church has shifted from the Northern and Western Hemisphere to the Southern and Eastern Hemisphere. What was once a faith dominated by Europeans and those of European descent has now become a Christianity whose population center resides in Africa, Asia and Latin America. The move of God in the twentieth and twenty-first centuries has restored Christianity to its global stature. The increasing diversity of Christianity reflects God's intention as evidenced by Micah 4 and Revelation 7. God's intention is for all the nations, peoples and cultures to gather before his throne in worship. In the twenty-first century we are allowed a glimpse (as imperfect as it may be) into the future promise and expectation of heavenly worship. The future of the church is evidenced by the demographic changes experienced by this generation.

While many will view this shift as a foretaste of greater diversity to come, these changes may also yield a fearful response from the people group that operated as the dominant group for many centuries. Those in a privileged position may respond in fear to protect the privilege that comes with the power of empire—the empire of Christendom characterized by the Western cultural captivity of the church. The story of European Christendom has dominated the narrative of Christianity for the past five hundred years. The demographic changes that are now deeply entrenched in the twenty-first century demand that the church embrace God's ongoing work. The church is called to delve deeper into faith and to challenge preconceived notions that reflect a cultural captivity. Toward that end, I would offer two biblical truths I have found to be helpful in my ongoing spiritual formation. I believe the church does well to remember the beauty of being made in the image of God balanced with the reality of human sinfulness and fallenness.

THE IMAGE OF GOD

All of humanity is made in the image of God. Human dignity is rooted in this reality. We must value the dignity of every individual, since every individual is made in the image of God. The image of God results in the gift of creativity endowed upon every human life. This creativity leads to the act of procreation as a means of reflecting the image of God. This creative capacity, however, is not merely evident in the creation of new life through procreation—otherwise, we would be no different in our creative efforts than animals. This capacity for creativity not only results in procreation but also re-creation. Creativity expressed through re-creation allows humanity endowed with the image of God to be expressed as cultural beings.

The great promise of the *imago Dei* found in all of humanity means that humanity in both the individual and corporate expression has the capacity for great beauty and good. Humanity has the possibility of reflecting the fullness of God's majesty and glory as created beings capable of further creativity. Cultural expressions, therefore, offer the possibility of expressing the image of God. The danger of an increasingly diverse Christianity is the upholding of one cultural expression of Christianity over another. One culture may claim that their culture more accurately reflects the image of God than another, even as we encounter Christianity expressed through many different cultures.

I once read a book in seminary that claimed that there were three gradations of culture. At the top of the heap was "high" culture—found in classical Western expressions of culture such as Bach, Rembrandt, Aristotle and other forms of European art and philosophy. At the bottom of the heap resides "low" culture—popular forms of culture represented by television programs, Michael Jackson, Bon Jovi and Andy Warhol. Somewhere in the middle resides all other forms of culture labeled "folk" culture—Native American jewelry, Korean drumming, African tribal dancing and so on. The cultural arrogance of this book offered the superiority of one cultural expression over another. It was assumed that classical Western culture would rest at the top of the cultural heap and dwell in a position of authority and preeminence over other cultural expressions. With new expressions of Christianity found throughout the world, the imperative for the next generation of believers is to seek and acknowledge the presence of God's image in all individuals and cultures. The ability to see culture as an expression of God's creativity, not just our own human creativity, should call us to honor the presence of God in every culture that we encounter.

FALLEN

However, the optimism of a people created in the image of God is tempered by the reality of the Fall. Fallen humanity, despite our unique endowment, suffers under the weight of sin. All of humanity has been affected by the Fall. Every individual lives under the weight of sin. Sin affects both the life of the individual and the formation of culture. There is no one righteous in light of the fullness of God's glory. There is no culture that should be elevated to any status or pretension of perfection. Human sinfulness permeates the individual and the creative efforts of the individual as expressed through culture. Cultural expressions can hold the majesty of God's image but also contain sinful human efforts.

The optimism of cultural expressions of Christianity arising from the image of God recreated by individuals and by communities must be balanced with the realism of the pervasiveness of sin found in every human expression. These two truths should be held in balance as we consider the move of God on earth. The church resides between these two truths of God's majesty and glory on one end and the reality of sin on the other. In between these two worlds, human culture resides and provides the ground on which the church operates. The middle in which we dwell should cause us to not exult too much in the beauty of human creation and to not dwell too much on human fallenness.

SHALOM

The ongoing work of God is to find the fullness of humanity in the middle of his image and in the context of fallen humanity. The gift of the *imago Dei* and the reality of the Fall provides the context for God's work. The gospel, therefore, finds itself in a serial expression. Missiologist Andrew Walls asserts that Christianity has always been a serial faith. New cultural expressions of Christianity rise up as a previous expression of Christianity diminishes in influence. The power of the Christian gospel is the power of translation. The linguistic and cultural translation of the message of the gospel in unique cultural contexts provides the vibrancy of the ongoing work of God. God does not change. The gospel does not change. But a changing world offers the opportunity for the gospel to be expressed in dynamic ways. The image of God is now revealed in new ways through the array of cultural encounters that are made available. With each cultural expression of the gospel, we get another glimpse of God's image through another lens. The fullness and completeness of God's shalom is made more and more evident as the gospel is expressed in multiple cultural contexts.

The twenty-first century offers the amazing opportunity to engage in the fullness of God's image. The fullness of God's creative act now expressed through the vast array of human diversity provides a great promise for the future of the church. The choice for the church in America is whether the richness and fullness of God's image will be embraced and celebrated, or whether our sinful self-absorption will continue to call us to extol the stories of our own communities at the exclusion of the stories of others. My admonishment, therefore, is to challenge the assumptions of a dominant cultural paradigm that calls for an exceptionalism that will conquer all other expressions of humanity. Instead, we must embrace the good work of God found in the expression of his image throughout the multiple expressions of Christianity throughout the world.

The Paradox of Peace

Tim Arnold

You will keep in perfect peace,
those whose minds are steadfast,
because they trust in you.
Isaiah 26:3

Peace I leave with you; my peace I give you.
I do not give to you as the world gives.
Do not let your hearts be troubled
and do not be afraid.
John 14:27

To *the Church of North America,*

One of the clearest promises of God throughout the Bible is the promise of peace. Yet, when we look at the average North American Christian and the state of the church, it is hard to find examples of this promise lived out.

On almost every corner we see churches with catchy slogans on their sign (e.g., *Running low on faith? Stop in for a fill-up!*). Yet so often, within the doors, instead of discovering a unified body of believers, we find a divided group of people who are much more focused on internal battles like organs versus drums, or whether wearing jeans to church is edgy evangelism or borderline heresy.

It's hard to drive more than a block without pulling up to a car proudly displaying the Christian fish or some other bold expression of their faith (e.g., *Canada needs a Faith-Lift!*). Yet so often the driver of the car could be described as anxious, depressed and bitter rather than harmonious, tolerant and peaceful.

Is the Bible simply wrong or untrue? Does its promise of peace no longer hold true in this postmodern age? Or have we missed something in our understanding of what *peace* means?

I believe that the Bible is as true and relevant today as it always has been. I believe that God's promise of peace is not just a promise for eternity but is designed for us to experience today. However, I believe this can only become a reality when we start to embrace the very thing that our upbringing has trained us to avoid at all costs—tension.

When people think of the word *tension,* they often think of aggression, fear, fighting and pain. As a result, tension is something we work hard to stay clear of. But this is where we have been deceived, and at the high price of our peace. In fact, tension can be a beautiful, healthy, even divine force that actually allows us to enter into a life of peace.

By definition, *tension* is a force that stretches an object, increasing its size or strength; it is achieved when two forces or values are opposing one another. An example of this is the opposing forces that make breathing possible. Our bodies have the ongoing need to take in oxygen; however, we also have the need to release carbon dioxide. As a result, we live with the constant tension between inhaling and exhaling, and ultimately this tension allows our bodies to grow healthy and strong.

Applying this on a day-to-day level, to live in tension means that we are deliberately tapping into conflicting values. Personally, we experience this ongoing tension in things such as managing work commitments with our home commitments. As a parent, I experience ongoing tension between gentle, unconditional love and tough love and accountability. In our faith we are continually dealing with this type of tension as well—for example, the interdependence of grace *and* law, and a lifestyle of both faith *and* works. These competing values, along with countless others, are part of our everyday lives and our faith. When we manage them well, we thrive—they bring strength, growth and newness into our lives.[3]

So if tension is a force that allows us to be strengthened and to grow, why is the church fearful of it? What created the myth in today's Christian culture that a life of faith is free from tension? I believe there is a clear answer: The church has an unhealthy fixation and addiction to absolute truth.

Absolute truth can be easily identified because the opposite of it is false. For example, we know that the earth is a sphere, not flat. This is absolutely true. Any argument or debate is futile. There is no need for tension in this equation. Similarly, we base our eternity on some absolute truths regarding our faith. They are a matter of black and white, right and wrong, good and evil.

Absolute truth is a real, important and powerful thing, and if in the end this letter undermines or devalues it, I will have done more harm than good. However, if absolute truth is seen as the *only* kind of truth, we've been set up for a life without peace. This is because there is another, equally important, kind of truth—*paradoxical truth*.

Paradoxical truth is easy to identify because unlike absolute truth, the opposite of a paradoxical truth is *equally true*. In fact, the two opposing views need each other to be healthy over time. Think of breathing: you'd be correct if you said we need to inhale to sustain life, and you'd be just as correct if you said we need to exhale to sustain life. Although the two forces are opposites, they rely on one another. Even more important, if we live with only one side of a paradoxical truth, we are destined for failure. It's as futile as deciding to only inhale or to only exhale—we're guaranteed to end up blue in the face.

From beginning to end, the Bible is full of paradoxical truth. Take Proverbs 26:4, for example: "Do not answer a fool according to his folly, or you yourself will be just like him." Yet, if we take this statement as absolutely true, we become the fool because we are ignoring the complimentary truth found in the very next verse. Proverbs 26:5 states, "Answer a fool according to his folly, or he will be wise in his own eyes."

And here lies the tension. We are now caught in a reality where the black and white of absolute truth no longer serves us well. This tension is unavoidable, unstoppable and unsolvable, and it's a key ingredient to a life of peace.

Let's be clear about what the word *peace* means. When we think of the word *peace*, it's easy to conjure up images of a person sitting quietly by a babbling brook in the middle of a lush forest with birds singing beautifully in the background. In church, when we talk of God's promise of peace it's consistent with this picture. This definition of peace is directly linked to absolute truth; it's the peace that comes from the assurance that you know that you know that you know. And although this perspective of peace is real and critical in our lives, it cannot be sustained without the other meaning of peace.

Peace occurs when a society or a relationship is operating harmoniously, and harmony occurs when two or more people, groups or things are free from conflict and working well together. This suggests that peace does not only come from having the "right" point of view; it also can result from a relationship between different points of view. There is an aspect to peace that comes by accepting, even embracing, tension.

It's not that the average Christian wouldn't concede to most of this conversation—so far. It's hard to argue the reality of the tension between grace and law or faith and works. But when push comes to shove, our default is to size up every situation through the black and white perspective of absolute truth; as a result we don't have the tools needed to access the peace that can only come through divine tension.

Christians today have become skilled at tolerance. To tolerate means to "endure without repugnance." If I believe that the liberal political platform is best, I can potentially tolerate people who don't share my views. I might even find the strength to pray that God will show those who disagree with me the truth he so graciously showed me. But this is a far cry from embracing. To embrace is "to take or receive gladly or eagerly, to accept willingly, or to hug." This means I can hold on to my liberal bias while at the same time entering into the tension of embracing the perspective of those who see the political landscape from a different, more conservative point of view. I now realize that I need to harmonize these two perspectives because if I get my way, I will ultimately lose out in the end.

Many Christians have lost the ability to embrace opposing perspectives. We associate it with giving up, giving in and selling out. The fears and vulnerability associated with losing the foundation of absolute truth render us powerless to go beyond toleration. As a result we live in disharmony with our opposites, and anything or anyone that challenges our views pushes us to a public or private state of anxiety, aggression and fear. Ironically, because of our addiction to absolute truth and our need to see the entire world in black and white, we end up living with the very negative attributes that we wrongfully associate with tension.

So the question becomes, How do we move from a lifestyle

and a faith that avoids and fears tension to one that embraces and understands it as a beautiful and divine force? The best word to summarize the answer is *diversity*. A life of peace should be synonymous with a life full of diversity: diverse relationships, diverse experiences and a faith that's open to diverse questions and perspectives. In the first thirty years of my life, I rarely swayed from the beliefs I was raised with. I generally stayed within my socioeconomic and Christian social group, and this dictated what I did and didn't do, where I did and didn't go, and what I did and didn't believe. This drastically changed, however, the day I met Wayne.

Wayne was a homeless man who, in the most unlikely of circumstances, became one of my best friends. He was the first truly different friend that I ever had in my life, and opening myself up to this friendship made the reality of paradoxical truth more real and unavoidable than ever. I was forced to question my absolute truths in regard to how God helps and heals people. My assumptions about people on the streets being lazy and needing to "just get a job" were challenged, and I had to examine the potentially unjust realities of some of the political systems that I historically supported. It made me tap into the tension of how the poor need the rich, and, to my surprise, how desperately the rich need the poor.

If you were to assess your life right now and look at the people you truly love and respect—whose views and perspective you truly embrace—my question is, Are at least half of these folks different from you? Does your inner circle of friends include people with different political perspectives, skin colors or sexual identities? Do you find yourself in meaningful, healthy and challenging dialogue with folks who differ with your views on Christianity, or who potentially don't even believe in God at all?

If you are privileged, do these people represent the realities of marginalization? I'm talking about going beyond serving in the food line of a homeless shelter: befriending someone who is homeless, going from wearing T-shirts that bring exposure to injustices in the developing world to having an authentic relationship with a newcomer to North America.

If the answer is no, then I fear that you are missing out on the awesome opportunity of embracing divine tension. If the answer is yes, do you simply *tolerate* their diverse perspectives, or do you *embrace* them, knowing they hold wisdom and truth you desperately need?

When you examine how you spend your time and money, would it be consistent with the average person in your church, or would it stand out as different, potentially even absurd? This matters because diversity goes beyond *who* we spend our time with; it also includes *what* we do with our time and resources. I have a friend who recently decided that instead of doing an all-inclusive beach vacation, he and his wife were going to use that money to travel to Guatemala and work with a humanitarian organization. The trip turned out to be life-changing, and recently my friend told me that since he returned home he feels he is constantly living in tension: tension that comes from enjoying and being thankful for the gifts and privileges he's been given here in Canada, while, on the other hand, starting to take responsibility for the poor and needy that he has the potential to assist. He said that sometimes the tension keeps him up at night, but he also said that he wouldn't trade it for the world. He feels more vibrant, more aware and more alive than ever. Surprisingly, living in tension is leading him toward peace.

Remember that by definition tension is a force that stretches an object. One of the best ways to deliberately go in the direction of peace is to look for a variety of things that are sure to stretch us and pursue them with all our might. Quite simply, the longer I keep surrounding myself with the same people, places, politics and perspectives that affirm my values, the longer I miss out on embracing the tension needed for a lifestyle of peace.

Since I've evolved in who I consider my inner circle of friends and how I spend my time and resources, I'm finding that everything is changing. I feel like I know a lot less, especially in terms of understanding God, yet I have never felt like I knew him more. I do not live with peace every day, all the time. But since my lifestyle of diversity has increased the amount of healthy tension in my life, I understand peace better and am realizing this promise of God more than I ever believed possible.

The church has been tricked into believing that the pathway to peace is found solely through absolute truth. We need to hold on to this value but realize that until we compliment it with the beauty of paradoxical truth we are destined for discontent. When we blend our need for the black and white of absolutes with the realization that the God of the Bible is also a God who abides in the land of mystery and paradox, we can finally begin to discover God's eternal promise of enduring peace.

On Self-Justification

Nathan Colquhoun

Dear Church,

In *The Hidden Wound* Wendell Berry brings up the example of the moral predicament of a master who sat in church with his slaves. In the church the master sits with the assumption that he can actually own the body of a person he considered as worthy of salvation as his own. This master is living a life that is completely contradictory. His actions say one thing; his beliefs say another.

My intent in this letter is to reveal the barriers of self-justification so that we stop flattering ourselves, revel in forgiveness and grace, and then begin to change to be more like what the kingdom values. Specifically, the separation between action and belief needs to be addressed in the church today. This separation needs to be addressed in my own life. For instance, I have a deep belief about food. I believe that it is right and good to eat healthy, organic, local food. There are many reasons why I believe these things; each reason is compounded by fact, experience and hearsay resulting in the belief that I now hold. Regardless, my actions do not always support my beliefs. Much of the food that I eat travels far before it finally rests on my plate. Sometimes late at night I snack on a bag of chips slathered in processed cheese. How can this be? How can my actions be in such drastic contrast to what I believe?

Psychology tells us that belief and action don't necessarily have to line up. A study by Theodore D. Wilson and Richard E. Nisbett had women come into a room and choose from four identical pairs of nylons. Every woman chose a pair and then was asked to give a reason as to why they made that decision. Over eighty different reasons were given. But those reasons couldn't be true because all four pairs were completely identical.[4] We have this dire need to justify our reasons for our actions, even when there isn't a real one.

The problem is that when we self-evaluate, we always have skewed judgment. We justify our own actions so that every decision we've made and every step forward has been a good and healthy one. We move very quickly from self-evaluation to self-justification. We always give ourselves the benefit of the doubt, make excuses for ourselves and eventually destroy any opportunity we have to ask ourselves if we were wrong, or if we made a mistake, or if we've been going in the wrong direction. Our indoctrinating techniques and discipling efforts have not produced disciples who are more intelligent or better Christians; rather they have only served to produce more confidence in our intelligence and our version of faith.

The church suffers deeply from cognitive dissonance, or the inconsistency between what we believe and how we act.[5] However, we also refuse to admit this inconsistency, so we try to change either the way we act or what we believe. This is self-justification at work, and we, the church, have chosen to change what we believe so that it will line up with the way we want to live. When Jesus told the rich man in Mark 10 that he had to sell everything and give it to the poor, the rich man was disappointed and walked away. He knew and admitted that his actions and lifestyle did not match up to his beliefs or what was expected of him. Can't blame him for trying—and try he did. He claimed that he had kept all the laws, and he'd done this and that. He authentically attempts to justify his life, but for some reason he has a hunch that there may be more. Maybe he had an inkling that all those things were not what was needed to have eternal life. When the rich man realizes that Jesus really does want him to sell everything, he walks away disappointed, because his actions could not line up. The rich man did not suffer from cognitive dissonance—he knew and admitted by walking away that his beliefs and actions could not work in sequence.

We, however, do suffer from cognitive dissonance. There are not very many people that I have met that think Jesus literally expects us to sell everything and give it to the poor. The plethora of excuses to get out of that belief is remarkable. We've seen entire prosperity theologies rise up in North America that are the complete opposite of Jesus' cut-and-dry instruction. Where are the movements of those that are selling everything and living with the poor? We justify our way out of these awkward commands from Jesus because we cannot translate this way of thinking into a rhythm for living. So, instead of changing the way we live so that it is consistent with our belief, we change our belief so it is consistent with how we are living. Why can't we simply admit that we believe one thing and act contrary to that belief? Why can't we live comfortably in that tension?

I wonder how many things the church has self-justified so that it doesn't have to live the way kingdom-oriented people should live, all the while pointing its fingers at everyone else for their poor decisions and secular lives. Selling everything and giving it to the poor? If you just have enough faith you'll be healed? Sunday services are the pinnacle of your Christian walk? Paid staff at churches should be the norm? Ten percent is all God asks of us? God is going to destroy the earth anyway, so we don't have to take care of it now? Evangelism is the most important role of a Christian? You only have something valid to offer on stage if you've written a book? Women shouldn't be in leadership? Sponsoring a child is a good way to fulfill our duty to the poor?

The church has a poor track record. I think I can say that without too many of us trying to justify our way out of the crusades. It's easy to refuse to justify something we didn't directly participate in, but what about things that we all do and participate in now? Are we justifying our way through life so we don't actually have to change?

My accusation is this: Most of the things the church holds dear are a result of self-justification and an inability to be humble or admit that we are wrong, living in the uneven tension between our actions and beliefs. We honestly believe that everyone else is crazy and we have it all figured out. The Catholics, Calvinists, emergents, Pentecostals, Muslims, gays, liberals, conservatives—they all have it wrong. They are all wrong, they are all completely ignorant, and until they believe what we believe about the world nothing can be right. This is a dangerous way to look at the world. When we can't give our neighbor as much grace and self-justification as we give ourselves, then we cannot expect to love them. When we can't admit that our actions are sinful and wrong at times, then we will be constantly changing what we believe to keep up with our feelings.

We need to stop being a self-justifying church and become a failure-admitting church, humbly accepting that we are all in need of God's grace because we are caught in bad systems that are hard to escape. It's not as easy to admit we are wrong, but nothing is gained by building systems inspired by our sinful lives. We tend to make morality and rules out of our justifications and our little mistakes. The problem is that it keeps escalating until we are allowing the worst of sins into our midst and creating systems to actually protect them. The early church would have laughed at the idea of Christians being wealthy; now we have entire movements telling us that God wants us to be wealthy and have everything we want. A switch like that doesn't happen overnight, it's a slow and systematic justification of allowing our beliefs to be shaped by our actions. The solution is not to believe the right things. The solution is to reverse the slow movement toward self-justification by practicing the slow-moving disciplines so our actions start to come back in line with who the church is and what it believes.

When we can admit failure, and say "My actions do not live up to my beliefs, but I'm trying my best," then we will actually start to see a reversal of the cognitive dissonance that has plagued the church. We will move from a self-justifying church to a failure-admitting church, and this is where we need to be. After all, I'm pretty sure Jesus only died for failures not those who have perfectly aligned their beliefs to match their actions.

Actually Living
the Truth

Kathy Escobar

Dear *North American Church,*

You have developed a bad reputation. I'm quite sure you didn't mean to. I believe your heart is good and you have been sincere in your dedication to Christ—of that I have no doubt. The problem is that somehow you've become more committed to *teaching* and *learning about* the truth than actually *living* the truth. You have focused on building successful businesses that are self-sustaining rather than living by faith and generously giving your resources away. You have spent your energy creating walls instead of bridges. You have dedicated yourself to creating programs instead of loving relationships with people.

The world has started to smell out your contradictions. You see, they are in need of hope and peace, not anger and control. They are hungry for love and cups of cold water, not hate and picket signs. They are desperate, dying, divorcing and deconstructing, and you are spending energy on trying to prove your "This is what the Bible says" point.

You have forgotten one of the most important things that Jesus beautifully modeled for us—he restored dignity to people who had lost it. The sick, the lame, the broken, the desperate, the outcasts, the marginalized, the least, the last. Over and over, he healed them, lifted their head and touched them with hope. Hope that the kingdom of God was available now, and it wasn't only for the learned, the put-together, the healthy or the strong and powerful. It was available for all those who were humble enough to admit their spiritual poverty and need for God.

I want to remind you of the powerful story in John 9:1-41, when Jesus heals a man who was born blind. In the passage the religious leaders spent an inordinate amount of time and energy on the theological implications of his blindness. They focused their attention on the minutiae and completely missed the most important part—*a man's sight was miraculously returned, and his dignity was restored.* The man who was healed had only one response to all of their questions—"I don't know. One thing I do know. I was blind but now I see!" (John 9:25).

Throughout the Gospels, Jesus cut through theological conventions and restored dignity.

Meanwhile, his hands and feet here on earth—the body of Christ, called the church—are more known for caring about theological minutiae than actually loving people. For stripping dignity instead of restoring it.

The world does not need any more dignity-strippers. We've got enough of that going on without the church's help. What the world needs are dignity-restorers:

- People who are willing to call out God's image in those that don't know it's there.

- People who are willing to sacrifice their own jobs, time, hearts and money to change systems that keep others oppressed.

- People who use their own power and privilege to make space for those without it.

- People who are willing to tangibly care for that one person who everyone else has given up on.

- People who see beyond gender, politics, religion, socioeconomics, and the long list of other things that divide and segregate us, and engage in deep, meaningful relationships anyway.

- People willing to commit to long-haul relationships, offering compassion and love to the hurting instead of trite advice or easy spiritual answers.

- People who will stand between the stone throwers and the one about to be stoned, and advocate on his or her behalf.

- People who touch the untouchable.

- People who see the best in others instead of the worst.

It's not going to be easy to make this change. A cool website won't do it. All the right answers won't do it. Going to the next great conference won't do it. Reading the newest best-selling ministry book won't do it. Cooking up new, trendy programming ideas won't do it. Putting the word *missional* on the tip of everyone's tongues won't do it.

To become known as dignity restorers, *you have to humble yourselves and give up all kinds of things you rely on to keep you safe, strong and protected.* You have to let go of being right. You have to dismantle systems that perpetuate inequality, money, power and control. You have to stop hanging with people who are just like you. You have to give up making sure you're the "us" and others not like you are the "them." You have to lay down your idols of comfort and worldly success.

However, before any of this can happen, *your own dignity must first be restored.*

You must get in touch with who you really are—who you were meant to be, not what you think you had to become to feel better about yourself. Jesus can heal you too. You can humble yourself and touch his garment, seek his ways and surrender to love. It's so possible. Healing and hope is available now, but it starts with humility and confession.

Here's the wildest part—if you won't, can't or refuse to do it, you need to know that *others will*. Actually, right now, others are. They are actively being "the church" instead of wasting time hashing over who can teach and who can't, who's right and who's wrong, who's in and who's out, and who's giving money and who's not. They are getting down to Jesus' business without the trappings of "the church" and doing a fine job at restoring dignity in all kinds of neighborhoods, cities and around the world.

But I have no doubt if all your resources, hands, hearts, eyes, ears, buildings, power, influence and hope could actually be channeled to restoring dignity in person after person after person, *the image of God uncovered in people, shining brighter and brighter, would dim the darkness of this world like never before.*

Dear and precious Church, the world needs you. It is crying out for hope, mercy and love. Step into who you were meant to be, a reflection of God's image as *dignity restorers.*

Interlude

Janell Anema (Age 21-22)

Dear Church,

You told me I wouldn't be alone, but when I'm with you I feel lonely. You give lip service to the popular clichés about community and fellowship, but you don't know the real me. You said we were committed to "doing life together," but your don't ask, don't tell policy toward my life outside of Sunday service begs to differ. So much for accountability. I just vomited in your bathroom because I'm clearly hung-over. Can't any of you smell my loneliness? Or at least the alcohol on my breath? Happy birthday to me.

Hiccup.

Dear Church,

I'm sorry it's been so long since I've written, but I guess I've been busy. I can't actually remember what it is that I have been up to, but I'm sure it was important. Forgive me? Thanks.

I know that I can always count on you to take me back, and I really appreciate that. Honestly, what else are you going to do? I don't even have to do anything except show up. And tithe. It is just too easy to rely on the fact that I can pass since I still "look" like a Christian.

See you Sunday. Maybe.

ART

Art and Exile

Makoto Fujimura

Dear Church,

I speak to you as an artist.

Our relationship with you has not been easy. Artists are often misfits, dwelling in the margins of your communities. They are often seen in the back pew, if they come to church at all, wearing black. Maybe they look menacing to you.

But many of us, actually, sit in the front. We volunteer and are first to be with the poor. You just don't notice us. Some of us are even up in front preaching—you call us pastors, but we consider ourselves artists of the Word. Some of us are crusading against the wrongs of the world. We can get the attention of the "kings" of this world because our songs are so popular.

But we artists are often exiled twice: once by the church, and then, because of our faith, by the world.

Our exile by you started a long time ago. In the late eighteenth century you began to believe that we needed rational categories to try to protect faith from reason. Reason began to win the battle in this false dichotomy, and the mystery of our being and the miraculous presence of God behind the visible were under suspicion. Ironically, this division fragmented the body of Christ and gave secularism its power.

In the resulting arena of the rational, the artist's task to fuse invisible reality with concrete reality also came under suspicion. An artist knows that what we can see and observe is only the beginning of our journey to discover the world. But you wanted proof instead of mystery, justification rather than beauty. Therefore you exiled artists to the margins of worship, while the secular world you helped to create championed us and gave us, ironically, a priestly role.

"Secular" powers took over the institutions created by the church's retreat from culture creation—they ask us to be gods in their museums, concert halls and academic arenas. In turn, you erected walls to shield you and your children from these "dark forces." Dear Church, did you forget that our Father in heaven owns all of the earth? You might have given the power of creativity back to Egypt and acquiesced to your captor Babylon, but the true and living God still owns all the powerful institutions as well as the hearts of critics and curators.

Artists still have an instinct for worship. But instead of placing quality artists at the core of your worship, you force us to operate as extras, as in, "If we can afford it, good. But otherwise, please volunteer." So now they must worship in the temples of the "unknown gods" of our time—the sterile, minimalist boxes called galleries. Rather than giving devotion, they have to become celebrity merchants, selling their goods.

Instead of offering themselves to the Giver of gifts, they have to become purveyors of a commodity.

Artists have insight into the invisible qualities of reality, but you have forced them to serve only the visible, the utilitarian and the pragmatic.

Artists have skill and power that dictators are either afraid of or want to use, and you, the church, unwisely neglected them. The first people known to be filled with the Holy Spirit were not priests, kings or generals, but artists named Bazelel and

Oholiab—it was they who built Moses' tabernacle. Even the Babylonian kings wanted God's artists after they conquered Israel, so they brought the artists to their land first.

God himself was, is and always shall be an artist, and he speaks through prophets and poets. The Bible begins with creation and ends with a new creation. Everywhere in between God has chosen broken vessels, his creative creatures, to create in love. What would he say about you exiling his artists? Perhaps something like this:

I AM an artist.

A painter does not merely reproduce what is thought to be seen by the eye. An artist's task is to train the eye first to truly see and to disregard previously imposed categories—those easy preconceived notions that lure us to think we are seeing when we are merely looking. An artist's task is to see through the eye into the eternal, into the invisible.

A musician's task is to hear, to listen to the sounds of the world. Bach, created out of the fabric of faithfulness to his community and to his church. He created through generational wisdom. He heard the echoes of the music of the spheres and sought to synthesize what he heard.

Do you not see what I see in a dancer's leap? It can never be repeated, even in eternity. Yet, eternity's echoes ring throughout the body, and I dance with them. Precisely because that act is ephemeral, I make them permanent.

A poet's task is to reveal through intuition the knowledge of reality and an emotional state that is at once mysterious but made accessible through her or his word.

One of your exiled poets wrote in 1864:

Love—is anterior to Life—
Posterior—to Death—

Initial of Creation, and

The Exponent of Earth—

Who is this love? Who is "anterior to life," and "posterior to death"? "initial of creation, and the exponent of earth"?

This poet, as a teenager, was told by your leaders in a seminary in Amherst that she was one of the "No Hopers," that she had "no hope to be saved." We know from these poems that Emily always desired to know her Creator. I do not celebrate waywardness, but I am here to seek the lost. I will leave ninety-nine church members to seek the one lost poet.

One of your exiled painters who lived in Arles, France, created a work called *The Starry Night* in 1889. In the middle of the painting a Dutch Reformed Church (that does not belong in Arles) holds the visual balance. Vincent grew up in the church. He even wanted to be an evangelist. But notice that the church is the only building in the painting that doesn't have light shining inside. He's trying to tell you through this visual parable that though the church still holds these disparate matters of the spirit and nature together in the world, the Spirit has left the church and went swirling into nature and the cosmos.

When you exiled them, the Vincents and Emilys of the world, you exiled me.

My artists: Create for me. Improvise with the Spirit. Create through the Medium who binds all things together, and then you will begin to hear sounds of "the world that ought to be." Surely, there will be birth pangs right up to that time. There will be more "Ground Zeros" created by destructive minds, twisting creative impulses into diabolical powers. Undo what they have done. Stand upon those ashes all around us, and open your hearts. Look up to create in love.

You, the body of Christ, must become as one and love one

another. Love is creative. Love is generative. Be diligent in the work of bringing unity in the diversity of the body. Art is unifying, bringing together diverse voices, instruments and colors for the magnificence of the whole. You are all God's masterpieces, a tapestry of diversity, created in Christ Jesus to birth more masterpieces.

Finally, you artists of the far country, you are starving though you have much. The corrupt world has given you celebrity and the ephemeral treasures of the earth. Return to your first love. Come home. Creativity is a gift. Don't make it to be other than that, or you will be crushed by it. And don't try to numb the pain you feel inside by drinking anything other than the Holy Spirit. The thirst you have, the longing that flows out of your own creativity, can only be met with the pure drink of the Holy Spirit.

There are also some of you in the far country who have removed pleasure from your life for the sake of "pure expression." Don't think that just because you have forfeited the whole world that you have gained your souls. Return to your first love and be filled with my passion. You used to explore the colorful margins, finding exhilaration in sound, movement, and rhymes of words. Come home and join me in preparing for the feast to come.

Dear Church of North America, do you not know that we are planning a wedding feast? Have you forgotten that? You are wedding planners! What wedding would lack music, art, poetry, dance or delectable foods? We need the best artists, poets, dancers, musicians and architects to prepare for the feast of grace when you will dance, sing, paint and create with the living God.

Dance with us, Church of North America. Join in the celebration of tasting what is to come and move to the enduring echoes of the ephemeral and the mysterious.

We Miss the Mark

Wendy Gritter

My Friends . . .

My friends who gather in the name of Jesus the humble One.
 Oh how I love you.
I love your devotion, your worship, your prayer.
I love your compassion, your concern and your care.
I love your celebrations and moments of joy.
I love you because we are one.
I love you with your blind spots.
I love you with your passions.
I love you with your half-assed and misdirected efforts.
I love you with your fearful strivings.
I love you because we are one.
Across the differences that mark the body of the striped and
 wounded One, oh how I love you.
Through crisis and tumult, factions and fighting . . . I love
 you.
Through dogmatic certainties and defensive posturing . . .
 I love you.
Through divisions, alienation, inequities and injustice . . .
 I love you.
I love you because we are one.

I love your dreams, your surrender, your service.

*I love you in your decline, your revitalization, your new
    initiatives.*

I love you with your professionalized shepherds.

I love you with your programs and strategic plans.

I love you with your huge buildings and budgets.

I love you because we are one.

*But oh how this love slays me. It cuts. It groans like a
    volcano waiting to erupt.*

*This love pulverizes triumphalistic expectation for
    transforming prosperity.*

*Such love is raw. No niceties here. No please and thank you.
    No limp-wristed handshakes.*

This love is pain and this pain is love.

*Such paradox, my friends, is the tension in which we are
    called to live, to hunker down and make our home.*

*But we don't want to. We don't want pain. We don't want
    paradox. We don't want conflict—even as we cause and
    create it.*

*We want . . . we demand resolution. We grab for our
    certainties requiring the conformity of all others who
    come through our doors.*

*Our systematizing elevates closing the logical loop and
    suffocates glorious mystery.*

*Our bifurcated days and bifurcated hearts consternate and
    call for perceptions of hypocrisy.*

We, my beloved friends, have missed the mark.

Our arrogance rarely leaves us.

*We sanctify our colonizing tendencies, calling it discipleship,
    blind to our own exclusionary demands of assimilation.
    "Become like us."*

We argue ad nauseam, and in our loveless debates trample

the lives of the real people the issues affect.
We fixate on sin and forget the words of the Master—
without mercy our sacrifice is useless.
Our cynicism dries up our gratitude, and we audaciously
demand more intense experiences.
My beloved friends, we have missed the mark.
No one likes to be told they've been patronizing, but my
friends how condescending we have been—across the
street, across the country, across the globe.
Our oblivion to the domination and power plays of our
majority privileged status render us oppressors of the
invisible kind. And we say, "Who us?"
We respond to the prophet from the margins with our power
of cash and programs—failing to receive the exposure of
our own impoverishment.
Oh my friends, we have missed the mark.
We talk with clever words of revelation and inerrancy and
authority as we make an idol of literal text.
We hold conferences and workshops and go to seminaries,
and we learn so much our cognition thwarts the
connectivity of imagination and spirit.
We strain to engage story, to glimpse living exposition.
But my friends, we miss the mark.
We capitulate to compartmentalized and virtual encounters
and struggle to enter the chaotic, intimate realities of
community.
We perpetuate favoritism and dishonor courageous difference.
Our privatized lives open doors for hidden escapes.
Our addictions and consumptions dull our minds and
deaden our spirits.
Our aloneness drives us to up the ante on risk and
recklessness.

Our houses are big, our homes are few.
Our world, the air we breathe, the water we drink, the soil
    we till pays the price.
Oh my beloved friends, how we miss the mark.
We preach on grace but live in fear.
We teach Trinity but Sybil-like split God.
We reach the lost but project our parched anxieties.
Beloved ones we miss the fullness of love.
Clanging gongs. Crashing cymbals.
What will enlarge our receptivity? Our capacity? Our
    generosity?
Our posture in weakness, humility, powerlessness . . .
This love is pain. This pain is love.
Come, make your home in this tension—this place of
    incarnation.
Heaven meets earth; earth meets heaven.
Poverty meets wealth; wealth meets poverty.
Exclusion meets inclusion; inclusion meets exclusion.
Injustice meets justice; justice meets injustice.
Doubt meets truthfulness; truthfulness meets doubt.
Fear meets hopefulness; hopefulness meets fear.
In these spacious, tension-filled places, listen for whispers,
    look for glimpses, sniff for fragrance.
Let eyes meet, gazes locked. Seeing anew, crossing borders,
    singing new songs.
Embracing suffering. Inviting obedience. Embodying shalom.
Humanity meets God. God meets humanity.
The fullness of love.

This Is an
Appeal to Zeal

Cyril Guerette

To the few . . .

To the few who are anew, the glue,
the true church in North America.
Let me be fair to ya . . .
Yours is a history of consistently spreading the Word of the
    Lord to the world constituency . . .
Yet I must insist that the unity of the community isn't just
    what we were, or persist to be . . . but what we wish to
    be . . .
Return to Your First Love . . .
Burn with the First Love . . .
Concerned to desire that Holy Spirit Fire.
And here we sit in North America, afraid . . . fearful.
The powers that be are not afraid of us . . . they smell our
    fear.
The average church in North America is dwindling . . . filled
    with older people, as the younger generation seems to
    turn from God.
And the younger generation who does hold on to their faith

*. . . they most often look no different than the world they
live in.*

*They are afraid to stand out. They live in spiritual sedation.
They fall into the paralyzing sins of intoxication and
sexual gluttony.*

*We cry about our own state, why would anyone want to be
like us?*

*We are not on fire . . . we are cold and lazy for the most
part.*

The church in North America needs to reacquire the fire . . .

Even if it's cheesy breezy.

Even if it feels lame . . .

It's time to pick up your zeal game!

*Never be lacking in zeal, but keep your spiritual fervor,
serving the Lord. (Romans 12:11)*

God's calling to the ballers,

to the slacker generation . . . stop slacking . . . you are lacking!

Get back for regeneration.

It's not okey-dokey . . . we've become so slow and poky.

Why the reluctance, why a reticence to act?

Struck by circumstance, we are hesitant in fact.

Shrinking away from thinking . . .

Shirking from working . . .

a lazy lack of drive and ambition . . .

Is just surviving our mission?

Instead of holding back let's take the bold track.

May our fear disappear,

Our dread of going ahead.

Today the Sloth doth let the moths eat up the folded cloth . . .

Slouching on the couch . . . immobilized in entertainment.

*We know the lies about self-gain are meant to destroy our
joy of Christ, the main event.*

A culture of kids whose greatest amount of action is spent
    pushing buttons, watching other people move across a
    screen. Living their lives vicariously through characters
    in a fabricated world.
Is it the goal of the church to surf the Internet idly, wildly
    for hours finding out tidbits of information about the
    most inane things instead of allowing the Word of God to
    penetrate and change their very minds?
Our culture is purposefully making us passive.
Let's get off our asses!
I don't know if the fluoride provided
Is meant to ensure we're always on the down-side . . .
But I look in our vicinity, and I see a nation of zombies
Whose only divinity is Comedy.
A couch-ridden bunch lacking all ambition.
This is an Appeal to Zeal.
Do not be lazy toward Zeal.
Do not lack Zeal.
Do not shirk the work of Zeal. . . .
Yet Zeal . . . it's kinda a done deal.
Zeal has been so attacked that it is labeled lunatic and
    crazy.
Being normal is being lazy.
A zealous Christian is our culture's most despised position.
Because we've seen zeal go astray, and that's instructive . . .
But if we have no zeal today . . . then we'll never be
    productive.
Zeal for an evil thing will be doubly destructive . . .
Yet lack zeal for the will of Christ . . . and we cease to be
    constructive.
So what's the deal with zeal? What is real zeal?
I submit it . . . Zeal is a quality of genuine commitment.

*Zeal is an expression of active concern, devotion, care and
    goodwill.*
Zeal is being earnest like a furnace.
Zeal is due diligence, in all its brilliance.
Really it's . . . being eager for the good, true and beautiful.
It's a believer being useful.
Zeal is all about effort and striving to accomplish.
Being alive and astonished.
*Zeal is doing one's best and not backing down no matter who
    is trying to stop you from doing the good you ought to.*
*When Jesus cleared all the bankers and money-changers out
    of the temple of God. . . . "Zeal for your house will
    consume me."*
Zeal made Jesus run the filthy profiteers out of true Religion.
*Jesus had zeal for his Father's house . . . Zeal for the holy
    temple.*
*But now WE ARE the temple of God. Our bodies are a
    temple for the Holy Spirit . . . and as a collective . . . as
    the body of Christ . . . WE ARE the temple of God.*
*Zeal for God's house consumed Jesus . . . and zeal for God's
    house should consume we who follow in his footsteps.*
*Continue Jesus' mission of zeal . . . our Zeal is for God
    himself . . . his temple . . . his body . . . his church!*
So when it comes to Zeal . . . don't be lazy.
Feel the zeal.
BUT KEEP YOUR SPIRITUAL FERVOR (Romans 12:11).
"TO THE SPIRIT . . . BURNING."
When it comes to the Holy Spirit . . .
we should have a fever of fervor!
A bubbling . . . a boiling up.
SEETHING in the Spirit.
Each believer a seether . . .

The temperature of the waters of our Spirit is to be hot . . . a
  lot.
I wonder if the church of North America got over itself . . .
    if it stopped wishing so badly to be cool . . . what would
    happen.
What would we look like if instead of being zealous to be
    cool . . . we were trying with all effort to be hot?
What if our faith-life were actually boiling?
"Lukewarmers are gonna be puked outta the Lord's mouth."
Does Jesus not deserve for you to burn in his Spirit at all
    times?
Jesus is the Deserver of your fervor.
But we get too self-focused:
"I just don't feel like God is around right now."
So what! Is he around? Yes!
Of course he is, whether you feel him or not.
All zeal . . . All fervor . . . comes from and is oriented to
    SERVING JESUS.
If it's not something you're feeling . . .
in serving will come revealing.
Here's a sure cure to endure purer . . .
Be a server with fervor.
Fervent servants . . . actual actors, not play actors.
 People acting in love and service of Jesus with zeal and zest,
    fervor and candor.
Do you want to have zeal? Serve God.
Do you want to have the fire return? Serve God.
But the rank file cry out that they're not BEING FED.
If you think that then you're being MISLED!
The church in North America has so much spiritual and
    biblical food that it finds itself sitting around
    complaining about the presentation and the lack of

variety while it sits getting fat and lazy on the couch!
The problem is really that we have an abundance of
    spiritual nutrients coming our way and we aren't really
    exercising them.
We have pastors and Bible professors and podcasts and huge
    numbers of radio shows and amazing books.
We complain there is nothing on the TV when we have
    hundreds of channels. We complain we have nothing to
    eat when our fridge is full. We complain we aren't being
    fed when we get solid biblical teaching in many ways
    each week.
The problem isn't so much that we aren't being fed; it's that
    we're not working off those calories!
We're not actually exercising our faith . . . just running our
    mouths.
May we in North America return to our first love.
Let us get up off the couch and look for where we can put
    our hand to serve.
May we make Jesus himself the center of our day and week
    instead of some glowing box whirling machine.
Let us repent of our sloth . . .
Escaping the trap of couch-slouching,
vouching for Christ again.
Our Christian life isn't about weekly attendance and
    institutional criticism . . .
we're making every day about serving the Lord in love.
The Spirit is here. He has filled this room.
Now is the moment you can be rekindled. Don't let it
    dwindle. The fire is burning. The Spirit
    yearning.
No more spoiling, or soiling, let your blood get to boiling.
As we step on in action . . . we find satisfaction.

As to zeal . . . not slothful (that would be awful).
As to the Spirit . . . on fire (our true desire).
As to the Lord . . . serving (for he alone is deserving).
When the year of the Lord appears, we will see hate fettered.
Now let those who have ears, hear the seers' Eighth Letters.

Real Rest

Aileen Van Ginkel

Come unto me,
all ye that labour and are heavy laden,
and I will give you rest.
Take my yoke upon you, and learn of me;
for I am meek and lowly in heart:
and ye shall find rest unto your souls.
Matthew 11:28-29 (KJV)

Dear *Church,*

These words are familiar to you, workers in the church in North America, and you likely go to a comfortable place in your imagination when you hear them. But I see that your understanding of work and rest is faulty. And so, if you hear these words of our Lord with soft violin music—or maybe even spa music—in the background, I urge you to turn to another station, because the music that goes with this verse is massive—it's big, bold and beautiful.

The problem is you understand *rest* to be a cease in labor, and the bigger problem I see in you is that you carry out your labor in your own strength, not in God's. You have great zeal and huge desire to work hard in God's kingdom, but most of you are going about it in entirely the wrong way. You're working more hours than you should, you're constantly skirting the burnout cliff—and maybe you've even fallen off—all because you keep laboring under the burden of your own yoke, instead of the one Jesus offers you.

Dear people of God, the rest that Jesus offers is not the kind you take on Sunday afternoons (if you're lucky) or the deeper relaxation you enjoy when you're on vacation. Instead, it's the *utter relief* you feel when you finally let go of the idea that you're in charge—that it's up to you to get God's job done. It's that sense of being lightweight yet thoroughly grounded that comes when you stop leading Jesus and start following him instead.

Your commendable zeal is too often mixed up with the urge to labor under your own yoke—a yoke made of all sorts of baggage that you've picked up along the way of life—and it's driving you crazy, and not only you but also all the people around you. Just think of the confusion, the fear and distrust that litters the path behind you in your own experience, and then extend that to the people you interact with.

Our Lord offers alleviation of that burden you insist on carrying; and the relief you feel as you truly trust in God, rather than in yourselves, will be shared by others who are able to see God working in you. Can you sense how much better it feels to know that people are relying not on you but on the God working in you?

> Come to me, all you who are weary and burdened, and I will give you rest. Take my yoke upon you and learn from me, for I am gentle and humble in heart, and you will find rest for your souls. (Matthew 11:28-29)

Let's go back to that music in your imagination. I told you it was big, bold and beautiful. (That's as far as I'll go in suggesting what it should sound like. Who knows, even spa music could sound that way to some.) This music is big, bold and beautiful because the invitation to take up Jesus' yoke is as big, bold and beautiful as creation itself. Jesus isn't asking you to take on something weak and useless; he's asking you to work with him in something that is hugely powerful: powerful in the sense of sharing in his power as an agent of creation, powerful in the sense of experiencing the Holy Spirit enlivening the strengths you were born with and taking them to extents you didn't dream were possible.

The yoke you take on when you accept Jesus' invitation (or, depending where you're at, obeying his command) is one that fits you much better than the one you've designed for yourself. Jesus knows your size perfectly; he customizes it to suit you exactly the way he created you to be.

This yoke is also lighter than the one you labor under when you work through your own power, because it's shared. The work you're being called into is one of partnering—joining with God in God's mission to restore creation to its original intent, picking up the mandate to cocreate with God in the power of healing and resurrection that comes to us in Jesus through the Holy Spirit.

The scope of work in partnering with Jesus in cocreation— that work you are called to as a human being, the work that stretches back to the beginning of human days on earth—is enormous. It's big enough to encompass changing diapers one day and writing a theological magnum opus the next. It's broad enough to include advocating on a stranger's behalf in the morning and then mending an outstanding rift in your marriage relationship that same evening. It starts with caring for nonhuman creation and praising the Creator for it as you step out the door, and it ends with your prayer for blessing on your dog when you walk back through that same door. There's no chance such work could be considered weak or useless.

Work that's this energizing doesn't drain you. It doesn't drive you to that burnout cliff. So look around you, people of the church in North America—where are you at in relation to that cliff? Are you really listening to Jesus' words? Hear them again:

> Come to me, all of you who are weary and carry heavy burdens, and I will give you rest. Take my yoke upon you. Let me teach you, because I am humble and gentle at heart, and you will find rest for your souls. (Matthew 11:28-29 NLT)

Is there not a tremendous freedom in knowing that you're a servant and not the one in charge? Do you get a rush in the prospect of throwing your very being into a project that's directed by the Lord of the universe? If not, then you're disconnected from the source of your calling—you've unplugged and broken the connection with Jesus. It's no wonder that you've fallen back into working under the weight of your own burden.

So fix that connection, people of God! Plug back in! It's not like you don't know how. You've heard about the importance of fellowship, spiritual direction, accountability groups and practicing the spiritual disciplines. And surely you wouldn't be in this kingdom-building business if you haven't at least once experienced the power of prayer to break through walls and move mountains.

But if you don't know how or if you haven't experienced that power, or if you just need a reminder, I ask that you always keep your connection with Jesus grounded in God's Word. You need this "steady stream of words from God's mouth," as one paraphraser of Scripture puts it, even more than you need bread. Keep your prayer focused on Scripture, and above all else, *listen*! Listen to what God is saying as you pray! Listen to what the Spirit is saying to the churches across all time and across all space!

And now listen one more time to Jesus' words about work and about rest—Jesus' words of invitation, strong invitation!—as I read them to you from Eugene Peterson's paraphrase of Matthew 11:28-29:

Are you tired? Worn out? Burned out on religion? Come to me. Get away with me and you'll recover your life. I'll show you how to take a real rest. Walk with me and work with me—watch how I do it. Learn the unforced rhythms of grace. I won't lay anything heavy or ill-fitting on you. Keep company with me and you'll learn to live freely and lightly. (*The Message*)

Interlude

Janell Anema (Age 24-25)

Dear Church,

So, I was in class today and I was assigned a paper about economics and the kingdom of God, and do you know what I did? I Googled "kingdom + of + God." I was raised in church. I have been digesting spiritual truths as long as I have been eating solid food, and I was twenty-four years old before I learned about the kingdom on the Interweb. Now and not yet realized! God's dreams for the world coming true! The mustard seed, the yeast, the pearl—everything is starting to come together, just as everything is falling apart, yet somehow I feel at ease. Why didn't you tell me about this before?

Don't you trust me?

Dear Church,

I can't believe that I spent my life in your revival tents and sanctuaries and you never mentioned the kingdom. You spent all your time teaching me Christianity like it was paint-by-numbers. You reduced the gospel to paint-by-numbers while the Lord has been painting the kingdom with brush strokes as imaginative and creative as our very lives, across the canvas of creation that spreads as long as the epoch of time. You told me to live in a right relationship with God, but all you ever taught me was how to do the right things and not do the wrong things. You kept the scorecard while you taught me how to win at religion. But faith is not a game. It is a mystical revelation, is it not? Were there never enough hours in a Sunday service to get to the mystery; to get to the kingdom?

Or do you not know? Have you not heard?

Dear Church,

I go online and I read the books and I sit in conferences, and I know now that I am not the only one who has experienced an unraveling over the last few years. For us, the unraveled, the red and blue letters of the Gospels have bled together and enlivened our faith, our hope and our love. Now we wax poetic about simplicity and the rich young ruler as we listen to Derek Webb on our iPods. We drink free-trade coffee in our reusable mugs as we make eye contact with our local homeless populations. We go so far as to congratulate ourselves for not literally crossing over to the comfortable side of the street, but so often we are still unable to put love into practice, to have our faith influence our praxis, because it is still foreign. I want to wear my Toms shoes—I just don't want to get them dirty. I want to be a new kind of Christian, but I have no idea how to exchange my outdated religious currency, particularly when it seems my local church is setting the rates.

It is so much easier to focus on doing the right things and not doing the wrong things, and I am good at this religion.

But I want more.

Dear Church,

I'll never let go, but I should warn you . . . my unwavering commitment these days is less about affection and more about allegiance. I would still feel lost without you, I'd be orphaned, but you have been more like a gang than a faith community. I learned the dress codes and the appropriate hand gestures during worship, and I speak Bible verses like passwords, gaining entrée into the inner chambers of evangelicalism.

So why is it that I commune more with Jesus when I am in the mountains, when I am reading C. S. Lewis, and when I am alone with my journal, than on Sundays when I'm with you? I don't want to be like Emily Dickinson, holding church alone in my garden, the peonies as my pews, and smelling calla lilies in lieu of taking Communion. Then again, maybe she was on to something. I want to be radically in love with Jesus, passionately submitted to a Father, intimately led by the Spirit. Church, I'm not convinced that you can provide a space for that to happen.

I feel like I'm running ahead of you, but I told you I'd never let go, so please give me something to hold on to.

Dear Church,

Apparently we aren't supposed to pledge allegiance to anything or anyone other than him. No stars. No stripes. No treaties. No task forces. Just to a king and a kingdom.

Are you coming?

HOPE

Open Secret

Ikenna Onyegbula

To All the Sons and Daughters of David,

To all the sons and daughters of David too afraid to again be
   Kings and Queens,
let this letter be the Lazarus story that resurrects your dormant
   dreams.

For, if it's true what they say, that you will become what you
   believe
and can be governed by what you state,
then life is so minutely connected that even our breaths can
   procreate;
and the conceptions you nurse in life will most likely doctor your
   future on earth,
so the question is not how you were birthed, but what you believe
   that you are worth,
and at the moment, the clock is ticking,
your unborn success is kicking,
trying to escape the infertile womb of fear that aborts your
   self-belief,
for your impotence of heart is doom,
but depressingly commonplace in a world where

the most sacred thing worshiped is a dead president's face;
but understand that the fight for your soul is of course a course
   more coarse than smooth,
and regardless of the lies we embody, the Holy Spirit resides in
   Truth,
so thus, fear not,
for prematurely you have despaired, but your contractions are
   from above,
so miscarry those doubts you bear, for you are not barren of Love.

Let this letter instill the joy that your tears have washed away;
Let the passion that is the Christ spiritually seduce you today.
Let this letter be given eyes, let it breathe through human lungs,
Let this letter let our Father know that we yearn to speak his
   tongues.
For all the sons and daughters of David too afraid to again be
   Kings and Queens,
let this letter be the Lazarus story that resurrects your dormant
   dreams.
Let this letter reminisce on the prayers that we prayed before we
   preyed
   on a face stained with Love, who cleanly forgave on our behalf.
Let this letter be a throbbing memory of the Merciful God we
   have.
Let this letter wear the sadness on which Christ's feet trod the
   ground;
let this letter comprehend the humility it took to wear that thorny
   crown
Minus the seven that we already have, let this eighth letter show
   we are one
   for God so Loved the world that he gave His only Son;
let this letter quietly bellow John 3:16 through all our strife.

*so that everyone who believes in Christ will never ever perish
. . .*

but have ever . . . lasting . . . life.

A Particular People in a Particular Place

Jonathan Wilson-Hartgrove

D*ear Sisters and Brothers in North America,*

I'm grateful for this chance to write you a letter. Truth be told, I've been trying to write to you for some time. Because I thought I had a lot to say, I started with a book. Some of you were kind enough to read it, and I was encouraged by your response to write more. But seeing that so many of you have so little time, I started writing articles—even blog posts. I cannot bring myself to tweet, but I have agreed to fly a couple thousand miles once a month to speak to some of you face-to-face. I've been hoping we might connect.

But now that I have the chance to write a letter, it occurs to me that this may be the medium I've been searching for all along. As Marshall McLuhan so memorably told us, the medium *is* the message. And my message, if it can be summed up, is something like this: *God has not given us a strategic plan to save the world, but has instead saved the world by inviting us into a community marked by communication as personal as a letter.*

The letter, I'm afraid, is a dying art in our culture. It has long been faster and easier to call a friend than to write them. To the extent that our communication is simply about the transfer of information, the text message is now preferable. This new form frees us from the cumbersome conventions of grammar and greetings and questions like "How are you doing?" which can only slow us down. And, truth is, however much we complain about being too busy, most of us don't really want to slow down. I have a Facebook page, and on that page there is a notice that I prefer to communicate via letter. Still, I write twenty electronic messages for every real letter. After all, I can stay in touch with a lot more people that way.

But this desire to stay in touch with more and more people is in tension, I'm afraid, with my vocation to be part of a community that witnesses to God's quite personal form of communication. That is to say, while hyperconnectivity around interesting ideas might well serve to sell more books, I am increasingly doubtful that our preferred modes of communication have the capacity to convey the good and true Word which was made flesh in Jesus Christ. When God wanted to proclaim good news to all the peoples of the earth, he struck up a conversation with a guy named Abraham and told a joke that made Sarah laugh before it made her pregnant. If we are to be about the proclamation of that news in our own time, a medium as personal and conversational as the letter might be the only way.

You can't start a letter without thinking about the address. To whom, in particular, am I writing? I've already called you my brothers and sisters in North America, betraying a conviction that, wherever you find yourself on this vast continent, you are connected to me (and I to you) through a faith we share and a grace that knit us together long before we knew who we were.

But lest our convictions become mere sentiment, let's be frank: I don't even know your name. This lack of personal knowledge makes my attempt to write you a letter somewhat false. After all, we write letters to those who, though they are separated from us by distance, are still so important that we cannot imagine our lives without them. I have such people in my life, and I write them often. I trust you will not be offended, dear reader, if I tell you that when I think about those people, you don't immediately come to mind.

Yet, if I take seriously the relationship we share by virtue of the adoption that makes us fellow heirs with Christ, I am challenged to think beyond my natural affections to those sisters and brothers and mothers I did not know I had until I became a part of this peculiar people called church. That this family includes you, whose name I still do not know, suggests that there is something more determinative than an idea called "North America" which unites us. If we could sit down to a meal together, we'd have more in common than democracy or network TV.

But if our identity as living members of Christ's body is to be real in this time and place called North America, I suspect that the spiritual reality which we sometimes call the "church universal" will have to be manifest in the particularity of a local community. Which is to say, though I may never learn your name, some others must. And they will, no doubt, be grateful if you are willing to learn theirs too. Not just their name, but also the unique story it signifies, along with the accompanying gifts and hang-ups, questions and concerns. Knowing one another in this way will take time.

So, we cannot be in a hurry. We cannot let our frustration with the church as it is, in the place where we are, deceive us into thinking that we will find a better church—or a better community by some other name—if only we can get away from the frustratingly difficult people whose names we do know. Nor can we be satisfied to carry on with people more or less like us who do not question our assumptions about the world and our place in it. To believe in a church universal, which is always manifest in particular relationships, is to know that God wants to meet us where we are in the most unlikely people. We do not "receive Christ" when we say some magic formula, but rather when we welcome the stranger into the places we call home.

I was raised by people who loved Jesus in a place shaped by evangelical revivalism. I know my education should have given me a critical attitude toward people who talk with an accent like mine about our "Lord and Savior Jesus Christ." But such an attitude feels pretentious. And nothing in my life has ever mattered to me more than my Lord and Savior Jesus Christ. So I am glad to be an evangelical. The liberating power of the Holy Spirit at the heart of our very American movement gave energy to the abolitionist movement, the women's suffrage movement, the civil rights movement and the antiwar movement. In a world at war, being an evangelical gives me hope that Christians can stand against the worst of the injustices that now plague us.

But I am also aware that this most American of religious traditions has tended to separate faith from the particularities of bodily existence here on earth. I grew up singing "I'll Fly Away" and "When the Roll Is Called Up Yonder." I knew that I was Christian when I chose to believe that Jesus died to save me from my sins. I was told that the main reason I needed to continue my sojourn in this old sinful world was so I could share with others the good news that they too could go to heaven when they died.

At the particular moment when I was growing up in the church, the activist energy of evangelicalism had converged with this disembodied spirituality to produce a peculiar form of political activism called the Religious Right. I was an earnest kid, and I wanted to do all I could for Jesus. So I set out to become president of the United States. This necessarily entailed going to Washington, where I arrived as a Senate page at the age of sixteen. Given my own limits and the decline of the Religious Right, I doubt I would have ever made it to the White House. I am certain, however, that I would still be trying to make a difference in the world for Jesus if I had not been interrupted by the presence of Christ in a homeless man outside Union Station.

As I look back on the significance of this interruption in my own life, I cannot help but recall that this homeless man was black. The Southern Baptist Church I was raised in bore the name Southern because it had insisted on keeping its slaves in the mid-nineteenth century. We had, of course, moved on by the time I came along. But people don't put up that kind of a fight without some serious thought. The justification for our Southern way of life had been an insistence that it was better for Africans to be slaves whose souls would go to heaven than free pagans who would die and go to hell. Thus the intellectual foundation was laid for a sharp division between the soul and the body. No amount of talk about discipleship or ethics was going to overcome this fundamental divide.

This is only my own story, I know. I am not trying to universalize it. But I share it to offer some of the context in which I have come to believe that God has not given us a strategic plan to save the world but has instead saved the world by inviting us into community. I know for others the experiences may have been different, but I also know from listening to others that we Christians in North America share this existential struggle to integrate faith and practice, what we believe with how we live. I'm simply writing as a fellow traveler to say that I believe God can work the miracle of this integration in us when we pay attention to the particularity of our relationships in the places where we are. My own work, then, is not about redefining American Christianity or writing a treatise to set North American Christians straight. I write, rather, to invite you into the adventure that is Christ's body, a universal reality that is particularly present in the peculiar people whose names you know (or will come to know) in the place where you are.

I can't imagine anything that would say that better than a letter, written to you for this particular occasion, and signed with my own hand,

Seven Dreams

Ron Sider

To the Church in North America,
From One Who Is Both Lover and Critic

My plea to the North American church is simple: Please, I beg you, get serious about following Jesus.

Vast segments of the self-professed Christians in North America are lukewarm, culturally conformed persons whose actual lives contradict their Christian confession. They are almost as promiscuous, almost as materialistic as their unbelieving neighbors. They commit adultery, destroy the environment, neglect the poor and file for divorce almost like their non-Christian friends.

Polls show that evangelicals get divorced at the same rate as the rest of society. Racism, sexual and physical abuse in the family, materialism and uncritical nationalism are widespread among Christians.[6]

People in the United States and Canada live in two of the richest societies in human history. But we spend almost all of our vast wealth on ourselves. Over the last forty years, as our incomes have increased, we have given an increasingly smaller percentage of our money to the church. The materialism powerfully and constantly promoted by billions of dollars of advertising has sunk deep into our souls. Much of the time we live as if we believe the advertisers who tell us that joy and fulfillment come through more money and more gadgets.

Another problem, the rampant individualism in the churches, reflects that of the broader culture. A century ago most of our churches believed and practiced (to some degree at least) mutual accountability. It was assumed that Christians' thinking and behavior should be shaped by the mutual discernment of the body of believers as they prayed and listened to the Scriptures together. When I joined my local Brethren in Christ church in Ontario in 1950, I promised as part of the membership liturgy to practice Matthew 18:15-17 and submit to church discipline. Today, most Christians assume that how they spend their money or act sexually is nobody else's business. The church has no right to specify and require moral standards for its members.

Whether the issue is sex and marriage or money, justice and concern for the poor, vast numbers of Christians simply ignore what Jesus taught. A widespread lukewarmness pervades many churches. People sing the songs and repeat the right words, but their actions suggest that Jesus' teaching is not really very important to them.

To some extent, of course, this has always been a problem throughout church history. The temptation to water down Jesus' radical teaching, to slowly conform to surrounding culture, has always been powerful. And Christians have regularly manufactured rationalizations for their failure to follow Jesus— whether the issue is sharing with the poor, loving their enemies or keeping their marriage vows. But repeated failure is no excuse for disobedience.

Already in the first century the problem appeared. In the letter to the church in Laodicea, John condemns their lukewarm Christianity. And his response shows how seriously God takes nominal Christianity. God, who prefers that they be cold rather than lukewarm, intends "to spit you out of my mouth" (Revelation 3:16).

Perhaps that is what has happened to European Christianity in the last one hundred years. For over fifteen hundred years, Europe was the continent where Christian faith was most widely embraced. Today, only about 5 percent of the people in Europe go to church. In spite of remaining vestiges of a former time of more vital Christian faith, Europe is overwhelmingly secular. I worry that the same thing may happen in North America in the next fifty years. Canada is already well on its way down that path. Unless the lukewarmness is reversed, the United States will surely follow.

That tragedy, however, need not occur. All we need to do to prevent it is to get serious about believing in and following Jesus.

I dream that the North American church would do that. Let me sketch the outlines of that dream—a quick overview of what I hope and pray will happen in the North American church in the next fifty years.

At the center of my dream is that in new and powerful ways large numbers of Christians would truly understand the biblical Christ and unconditionally surrender their lives to him.

Something utterly amazing happened in a little corner of the Roman Empire two thousand years ago. A Jewish carpenter claimed to be the long-expected Messiah, got crucified for his radical social views and blasphemous claims, and then was reported to have risen from the dead. Equally astounding was that rigorously monotheistic Jews (the least likely people in the first-century world to say that a Nazarene carpenter was true God) almost immediately began telling everyone that

Jesus was God—the one to whom every knee should bow. Apparently the only possible explanation for the amazing events of Jesus' life, death and resurrection was for strict Jewish monotheists like Saul of Tarsus to conclude that Jesus was truly God in the flesh.

Also centrally important was their understanding of the implications of the fact that Jesus was the long-expected Messiah. The messianic kingdom—when sins would be forgiven in a new way and justice and peace would prevail on the earth—had visibly and powerfully broken into our history in the work of the Nazarene carpenter. In the power of the risen Jesus and the Holy Spirit he had left with them, Jesus' disciples were now able to live out Jesus' radical kingdom ethics, sharing with the poor, loving enemies and keeping marriage vows. Jesus' radical new community, the church, was a visible proof that Jesus' messianic kingdom had already begun and that Jesus would keep his promise to complete the victory over Satan and restore all creation to wholeness at his return.

As a result, the early church (in spite of failure) truly lived like Jesus, challenging the status quo in radical ways. The church was an astonishing new community where the rich shared with the poor. Jews accepted Gentiles, masters treated their Christian slaves as brothers and sisters in Christ, and men embraced an astonishing new equality for women.

I hope and pray that tens of millions of North American Christians will rediscover this full biblical Christ—confessing the Nazarene carpenter and resurrected Lord as true God and true man and inaugurator of the messianic kingdom. As a result, they surrender every corner of their lives to this glorious God and Savior, daring in the power of the Spirit to live now his radical kingdom ethics.

Second, I hope and dream that vast numbers of Christians

will become far more profoundly biblical in their thinking. George Barna has discovered that only a small fraction of today's confessing Christians have a deep understanding of biblical teaching. He also shows how profoundly shaped they are by societal relativism, especially postmodernism. Christians know that Christ is the way, the *truth* and the life. Jesus' story and teaching are not one of many equally valid ("true") ways to view the world. They are the truth about reality. Postmodernism's radical relativism fundamentally undermines Christian faith and practice. We need to recover John's teaching that orthodoxy (right theology) and orthopraxis (right practice) are equally important (1 John 2:22-25; 3:4-10). Only a massive return to deep biblical understanding that in turn nurtures a vigorous biblical theology and faithful biblical living can reverse the tide of surging secularism in North America.

Third, I dream of a revitalized North American church where the typical congregation embraces holistic ministry, combining evangelism and social action so they love the whole person the way Jesus did. For much of the twentieth century there was a ghastly division in the church between Social Gospel folk, who majored on societal peace and justice, and evangelicals, who focused almost entirely on evangelism. In the last few decades, thank God, evangelicals have rediscovered the biblical mandate to seek economic justice and care for creation. God bless today's younger Christians who have social action in their DNA. But I worry about whether they are losing the biblical balance: Do they care as much about leading non-Christians to the Savior as they do about overcoming poverty and environmental degradation?

I dream of a time when the typical congregation each year leads dozens of people to confess Christ for the first time—and at the same time is vigorously engaged in correcting injustice, working for peace and restoring the air, land and water for our grandchildren. I dream of a strong North American church discovering how to become true partners in mission with the majority church in the Global South. That kind of North American church would give sacrificially of its vast wealth to strengthen evangelism and foster justice everywhere in a way that truly abandoned the attitudes of Western colonialism and embraced mutual listening, learning, partnering and accountability in the one global body of Christ. That kind of global Christian partnership could dramatically reduce poverty, injustice, conflict and war, renew the environment and foster an explosive global expansion of servant evangelism.

Fourth, I dream of a North American church that takes the lead in combating our most pressing societal problems. Racism (including fear of immigrants who are not "just like us") is still alive and well in our continent. There is substantial poverty here and devastating poverty abroad that we do so little to correct. And Canada and the United States contribute (in per capita terms) a hugely disproportionate share of the carbon emissions that will produce devastating climate change for future generations.

I dream of a North American church—not just its leaders but tens of millions of laity—that become the vanguard to persuade our wealthy, materialistic societies to change. The richest nations in history could do vastly more to reduce poverty and disease around the world. Canada and the United States must take the lead in reducing carbon emissions so that the whole world will make the decisions necessary to pass on a decent world to our grandchildren. Imagine the impact on the larger society if tens of millions of North American Christians used their voices, their personal economic choices and their votes to persuade business leaders and politicians to make the necessary painful decisions.

Fifth, I dream of a North American church that repents of its sexual infidelity and marital disobedience, and returns to biblical standards on sex and marriage. Let's be honest. The church in my lifetime has largely followed the world in this area. Unmarried Christians are almost as sexually promiscuous as their unbelieving friends. Christians—including evangelicals—get divorced at the same rate as everyone else. Divorce has devastated the lives of our children. The result is agony and hell in our homes. This generation of parents has done to its children what no generation has ever before done to its offspring. I doubt that a decent society can long survive in North America unless we reverse the level of pain and agony in our homes.

I dream of a church that follows biblical standards. I imagine tens of millions of Christian families that live such a joyful, winsome model of wholesome family life and lifelong marriage that unbelievers are attracted to Christ. I dream of churches where youth wait until marriage to enjoy God's wonderful gift of sex, and married couples keep their marriage vows. I dream of marriages where husband and wife practice mutual submission, where they place parenting above money and career, and where they seek Christian counseling to help them through the inevitable challenges and struggles that invade even the best of marriages. That way, Jesus' way, I am convinced, is not only a biblical mandate. It is also the way to lasting joy and fulfillment. In the long run it leads to greater happiness than the life of temporary thrills that come from promiscuity. If tens of millions of Christians truly lived this way, our joyful, wholesome marriages and families would be one of our most effective means of evangelism. Christian marriages and families would be like a cozy living room heated by a warm fireplace in a frigid city frozen by a raging blizzard. Millions of hurting people would seek the same joy.

Sixth, I dream of a church that embraces a biblical balance in its concerns and activities—especially its political engagement. Politics is not all that important. It is not as important as evangelism. It is not the only way to change the world. On the other hand, it is significant. Political decisions in North America affect the lives of billions of people in our world. Wise political engagement is one way we love our neighbors.

But if Christians are to be engaged politically in a way that is shaped by Christ, then they must ask: What should we promote in our political engagement? Surely a crucial part of the answer is that we should be concerned with the things that God cares about. And when we turn to the Bible to see what God cares about, it is quickly clear that God cares about the sanctity of human life *and* economic justice, sexual integrity *and* peacemaking, wholesome marriages and families *and* creation care. A biblically balanced political agenda must be

- pro-life and pro-poor
- pro-family and pro-peacemaking
- pro-sexual integrity and pro-creation care

I dream of a church that does not expect too much or too little from politics and that courageously embraces a biblically balanced agenda even when some parts of that agenda displease significant segments of the larger society.

Finally, I dream of a North American church that dramatically overcomes the ghastly church divisions that have sapped its strength for centuries. Not very long ago, Protestant, Catholic and Orthodox Christian leaders said very awful things about each other. And we virtually never cooperated or even talked to each other.

Our divisions make a farce of Jesus' last prayer in John 17. Jesus prayed that his followers would be one, that they would be brought to complete unity, "then the world will know that you sent me" (vv. 20-23). Rather than drawing non-Christians to our Lord, our divisions and battles have caused people to turn away in disgust.

I wish I knew how to resolve the major theological disagreements among Christians today. I do not, although I believe we must keep working at that. But in the meantime we must put far more emphasis on where we agree than on where we disagree. Protestants, Catholics and Eastern Orthodox (at least those who still affirm their historic creeds) all believe that Jesus is true God and true man; that our one God is Father, Son and Holy Spirit; that Jesus' death is the only way to salvation; that Jesus rose bodily from the dead; that he will return someday to complete the victory over sin, injustice and death; and that the Bible is God's unique, special, fully authoritative revelation. That represents a lot of common ground.

Furthermore, if we look at recent major political agendas of evangelical, Catholic and Orthodox Christians, we also see a great deal of common ground on public policy. They are all pro-life and pro-poor, pro-family and pro-peacemaking, pro-sexual integrity and pro-creation care. Of course there are differences. But the common ground is huge.

I dream of a North American church that discovers in dramatic new ways how to focus primarily on what we have in common among evangelical, Catholic and Orthodox Christians. That kind of church would work together sharing the gospel and shaping society far more than we do. That kind of church would grieve over our continuing divisions and search vigorously for ways to transcend our ongoing disagreements. That kind of church would—by its growing unity—convince many unbelievers to embrace our Lord.

My friends, that is the church I long for and dream about.

And I think that at its core my central longing is finally that the Christians—vast numbers of Christians—become deeply serious about following the full biblical Christ.

The contemporary Christian song (inspired by Celtic Christianity) puts it well:

Jesus, be the center,
Be our source,
Be our light, Jesus

Jesus, be the center,
Be our hope,
Be our song, Jesus

Be the fire in our hearts,
Be the wind in our sails,
Be the reason that we live,
Jesus, Jesus

Jesus, be our vision,
Be our path,
Be our guide,

Jesus.*

---

*"Be the Centre" by Michael Frye, ©1999 Vineyard Songs (UK/EIRE) (PRS). Administered in North America by Music Services. All rights reserved. Used by permission.

Bigger Banquet Tables

Rachel Held Evans

To the Church in North America,

I write to you as one of your own at a time when many in my generation have abandoned you. As the church in the Third World continues to grow, the church in North America is in decline. Some are predicting our imminent demise, while others foresee a glorious rebirth. Most seem to think that we're in the midst of an identity crisis, one that will determine the shape and direction of the North American church for many years to come.

According to the statistics, we are a people of relative prosperity and relative generosity. We control most of the world's wealth and we give much of it away. Though we struggle with materialism, we value charity. While we want to make the world more just, we don't always know how to start.

But are we people of the kingdom?

That is the question at the heart of this crisis, and as we struggle together to answer it, I am convinced that we don't need bigger buildings or fancier sound equipment, better pastors or more parishioners, newer ministries or deeper pockets.

What we need are bigger banquet tables.

Jesus loved banquets. He performed his first miracle at a wedding reception in Canaan, turning jars of tepid water into the finest of red wines. He spent so much time feasting in the homes of sinners that the religious wrote him off as a glutton.

When the five thousand were hungry, he served them fish and bread. When the time of his death drew near, he ate dinner with his closest friends. After Peter had denied him three times, he offered redemption over breakfast. It's as if Jesus knew his message would mean more to us if we could taste and smell it. How fitting that in his absence we remember him by eating together.

When Jesus returns, he plans to throw a great banquet in honor of his bride, the church. It's an event foreshadowed by the prophet Isaiah who describes it as a

> feast of rich food for all peoples,
> a banquet of aged wine—
> the best of meats and the finest of wines. (Isaiah 25:6)

The apostle John called it the "marriage supper of the Lamb." Baptists call it one eternal potluck.

We get to enjoy a foretaste of this meal through the communion of the kingdom. Jesus compared the kingdom to a lot of things, but one of his favorite metaphors was that of a feast. "People will come from east and west and north and south," he said, "and will take their places at the feast in the kingdom of God" (Luke 13:29).

But while everyone is invited, not everyone will come.

Jesus compares the situation to a king hosting a dinner party. Just as the meal is about to be served, all the rich neighbors cancel, saying they've got too much to do. So the king tells his servant to "Go out to the streets and alleys of the town and bring in the poor, the crippled, the blind and the lame. Go out

to the roads and country lanes and make them come in, so that
my house will be full" (Luke 14:23).

Likewise, when we throw parties, Jesus tells us to invite the
poor, the crippled, the blind and the lame so that we too will be
blessed.

I suspect that Jesus used all this delicious imagery because
he knew that there is a difference between feeding people and
dining with people.

Feeding people means keeping the hungry at arm's length. It
means sending checks now and then, making thanksgiving
baskets once a year, preaching about justice, and launching
new ministries—all while sitting comfortably at the head of a
tiny table, dropping scraps of our abundance to the floor.

Americans are good at feeding people.

But dining with people is an entirely different matter. Dining
together means sitting next to one another and brushing arms,
passing the bread basket and sharing the artichoke dip. It means
double-dipping and spilling drinks, laughing together and crying together, exchanging stories, ideas, recipes and dreams. According to Jesus it means leaving the seat at the head of the
table ceremoniously empty so that all are guests of honor and
all are hosts. Dining together isn't charity; it's friendship.

For the church in North America to grow in a good way, we
need to break down the distinction between those who serve
and those who are served. The abundance must truly be shared.
At the local level this may mean hosting literal banquets, complete with Jesus-style invitation lists. At the global level, it
means sacrificing some of our own comforts so that when we
care for our faraway neighbors we can still feel their presence
beside us at the table.

In every case, it means slowing down long enough to savor
both the food and the company. It means admitting that we

need our neighbors as much as they need us.

So let's build bigger banquet tables.

Let's eat fruit that's in season and drink coffee that's fairly traded so that Latin farmers can join us at the table with their heads held high. Let's share the reputation of Jesus and dine with those who the religious love to hate—gays and lesbians, divorcees, single moms, junkies, dreamers and doubters. Let's squeeze in a little tighter to make enough room for people of all political persuasions, all religious backgrounds, all ethnicities and all denominations.

Let's eat a little less so that everyone has enough, and let's linger longer so that everyone gets a chance to share what's on their mind. Let's invite the poor, the crippled, the blind and the lame so that our house will always be full.

A Dozen (or So) Flags
and Seven Piles of Poop

Shane Claiborne

Dear Church,

First a disclaimer. In my Bible the words of the seven letters in Revelation are printed in red letters, indicating that they come directly from the mouth of God, so writing an eighth letter is an ambitious undertaking, even pretentious. I want to make clear that while I did my best to listen to God and ask the Spirit for help here, I should not pretend the words of this letter are written in red but black, and maybe even in pencil.

Second, a word of clarity. In the letters of Revelation, there are some pretty sweet images of seven stars, of golden seals, of seven golden lamp stands and such. I decided to run with the imagery here—I will use seven piles of poop as one metaphor of the potential messes, the things to avoid, things we sniff out lest we step in them. After the seven piles of poop, I'll offer a dozen flags to salute pointing toward heaven, and toward healing. So I hope you can smell what I'm smelling and salute the flags I'm raising. On that note . . .

To the angel of the church in North America and to all the saints and sinners therein: Keep your eyes open and keep your nose alert. There are seven piles of poop I want to make sure you don't step in.

Beware counterfeit gospels. Beware the false gospel of America's civil religion, which proclaims America as God's messianic force to be reckoned with, which proclaims America as a divine beacon of light to the world, the last best hope on earth. Beware "God bless America" Christianity, and let us remember that the Bible never says God so loved America, but that God so loved the world. If it does not have Jesus and the cross at the center, it is not the gospel of our Lord. Also beware the self-centered, blessing-obsessed gospel of prosperity, which is about what we can get from God. Be careful, amid all the terrible Christian books obsessed with finding our life and becoming a better you, that we do not lose the secret at the heart of Jesus—which is if you want to find your life you've got to give it away. We are made to live for something bigger than ourselves, the kingdom of God. If the gospel we hear is not good news to the poor, then it is not the gospel of Christ.

Beware the sins of Sodom. As the prophet Ezekiel said, "Now this was the sin of your sister Sodom: She and her daughters were arrogant, overfed and unconcerned; they did not help the poor and needy" (Ezekiel 16:49). Arrogant. Overfed. Unconcerned. Beware of these sins lest they suffocate your souls. Let's not boast of America the beautiful but of the glory of the cross. In a culture with an epidemic of obesity, let us fast and hunger for justice, for as long as we live in patterns of consumption—the average North American consuming the same as five hundred Africans—it is impossible to love our global neighbor as ourselves. Amid a world of numbness and complacency, pray that God would give us the gift of discomfort, that the suffering of others might keep us up at night.

Beware sloppy liberalism. Many of us were raised in a legalistic "don't do this, don't do that" Christianity that has left a bad aftertaste. Our instinct is to run the other way and create communities that are safe and tolerant and inclusive—and utterly undisciplined. This murky liberalism can lead to a sloppy spirituality. We must be deliberate to create holy habits and disciplines that cultivate goodness—both when it comes to orthodoxy and orthopraxis (right belief and right practice). There is also a lot of bad theology out there, but the answer to bad theology is not no theology—it's good theology. Do not throw out the core tenets of our faith, things like the bodily resurrection. Be vigilantly orthodox. And do not throw out the core practices of our faith, like prayer and caring for the poor, healing the sick, visiting those in prison and welcoming the stranger. Remember that *disciple* shares a root with *discipline*, and without discipline we raise up spiritual brats.

Beware the obsession with cultural relevancy. Certainly, our faith must address the deep hungers of the age—we must read the Bible in one hand and the newspaper in the other. You want to be relevant to the world you live in, but you must be relevant nonconformists. It is just as important to be peculiar as it is to be relevant. Consider the witness of the Mennonites—the world is poised for a new Anabaptist movement, for people have grown tired of materialism and war, and have begun to doubt the lies that happiness must be purchased and that violence can bring peace. Relevancy does not mean we are hip—it can mean we are a contrast society. Live in ways that do not compute to the patterns of the world, and love in ways that don't make sense.

As perhaps one example, the world is obsessed with big—supersized fries, cars and cathedrals. You can see in the megachurch that as we grow numerically we tend to lose the very thing we long for: community and love (so all the curriculum coming out of the megachurch is about getting people into small groups!). In the wake of the megachurch, there is a new movement of microchurch. We are to live small, like the mustard seed, the yeast, the leaven; we are a subtle infection of grace. Remember that small is beautiful. Grow smaller and smaller as you take over the world.

Beware virtual community. Everywhere you look there will be virtual revolutions, virtual networks, virtual friends, but virtual also means "almost real." Virtual relationships come without any responsibility or accountability, which is what makes them dangerous. There is a word we have for intimacy that comes without any obligations or responsibilities—*infidelity.* So don't replace real community with virtual community. The person with many virtual friends is likely to be very lonely. You will see that often as we connect virtually to the world, we lose connection with the people right next to us. We gain the whole world and lose our soul. If we only eat virtual food we will starve to death.

Beware polarization. Remember that just as important as being right is being nice. See your critics as your best teachers. Even if 90 percent of what they say is false, that means 10 percent is true—so look for the truth, and it will sharpen you in ways your friends don't. Be nice. Look at both the liberals and the conservatives and you can see that having good ideologies and arguments is not enough—you can have great ideas and still be mean and arrogant, and no one really likes listening to mean people. It makes for good TV, but doesn't look much like our Lord Jesus. Remember that anyone can be set free, both oppressed and oppressor, and don't forget that our Lord's Table has room for both zealot and tax collector.

Beware empty ideologies. Ideologies are like doctrines: they may be important, but they are hard things to love. And ideologies do not demand anything of us. Ideology must be accompanied by embodiment. Right living is just as important as right thinking. Your best argument is your life. What is just as important as what you believe is how you believe—if you are going to make a case against abortion, which I hope you do, you had better have some foster kids living in your home and you had better be caring for some teenage mothers. Otherwise all we have is ideology, and ideologies are hard things to love. We should be known for what we are for more than what we are against. Too often we have been known for what we hate rather than what we love.

And there are a dozen (or so) flags I want you to salute with me, for they point toward heaven.

Rediscover the art of spiritual formation. In the past few decades our passion for evangelism has come at the cost of discipleship. Our megachurches have left us with a Christianity that is a mile long and an inch deep. We have created a church of believers, not disciples. But let us remember the great commission sent us into the world not to make believers but disciples.

Remember your roots. Without roots we are like the seed that shoots up but dies quickly. The future of the church lies in remembering our past. Look back as we look forward. For this reason we have created a prayer book called Common Prayer (see commonprayer.net) to help remember the heroes and sheroes of our faith, and to remember dates in history that we dare not forget. Sing old songs, not from the 80's glam rock but from 800 years ago.

Embrace suffering. Everything in the world teaches us to move away from suffering and insulate ourselves from pain. We are taught to move away from neighborhoods where there is high crime or where there are people who don't look like us. But the coming of Christ is all about God moving into the neighborhood, one in where folks said nothing good can come. Christ knew suffering from the moment he was born as a refugee from Herod's genocide until he died on the old rugged cross. It is this Christ we are called to follow. Undoubtedly, some suffering is not to be embraced, like a woman being beaten by her husband—that is stupid suffering that we should expose and extinguish—but suffering that is born of the desire to bear the burdens of the world as Christ did is suffering that is redemptive. So locate your lives in a place where you encounter the pain. And beware of suburban sprawl, gated neighborhoods and national borders. These are dangerous things. And remember demons live not simply in the slums and ghettoes, but in the shopping malls and department stores. And it is not simply enough to care about the poor; we must know the poor. It is very fashionable to talk about the poor but not as fashionable to talk to them. And the great tragedy in the church is not that rich folks don't care about poor folks but that rich folks don't know poor folks.

Be fearless. Laugh at fear and death. Remember that our Lord looked death in the face and made a spectacle of it by his glorious resurrection. It is hard for the world to be convinced of resurrection when we Christians live in fear of death and are infatuated with security. Of all people we should be willing to risk death for love; people who would rather die from our enemies than kill them; people who know that even if we are killed, we will rise again.

Make sure that Jesus and justice kiss. Beware a gospel that is only social. And beware a gospel that is only personal. Over and over we overcorrect ourselves and end up creating a church of Jesus disciples without justice or justice disciples without Jesus. But loving God and neighbor cannot be separated. Our God is personal. And our God cares about the whole world.

God is healing broken lives and a broken world.

Proclaim a consistent ethic of life. Be known for being for life and against death. Remember that we follow the Way, the Truth and the Life. Get in the way of everything that destroys life. Stand with those who are oppressed. Interrupt injustice with grace. Be consistent and allow a consistent ethic of life to inform how you feel about abortion, the death penalty, war and militarism, poverty and prejudice. Christians should be the hardest people in the world to convince that violence is necessary. Remember the words of the early Christians: "For Christ we can die, but we cannot kill." There is something worth dying for, but nothing in the world worth killing for. Perfect love dies, but it does not kill. The moment we kill, we, like Peter, betray Christ. And the moment Jesus disarmed Peter, he disarmed every one of us.

Be creative. Be creative with your lives and with your words. Create ways of disarming your critics and making them friends. Abandon stale language and polarizing words. Rather than try to reclaim outdated labels like "pacifist" and "social justice," consider creating new language. Champion the nonviolence of the cross without using the word *pacifist*, for then you only end up preaching to the choir. Rather than getting stuck in the social justice war, talk about the *restorative justice* of the Bible, about how God is not just trying to give people what they deserve but set things right again and create restoration where there has been division. In this way we can move closer to the restoration of God rather than win the social justice debate. Just as charity without justice falls short, justice without reconciliation also falls short. Create holy mischief and prophetic stunts that invite people to hear the gospel in fresh ways.

Evangelize by fascination. Rest assured that the gospel spreads best not through force but through fascination. Live in ways that woo people to God. Contemplate the fruits of the Spirit and pray that they would live in you. Adore Jesus so much that he rubs off on you.

Avoid sectarianism. Just because we don't agree with someone doesn't mean we can't work together. Jesus used a Samaritan as the hero of his story. God can speak through pagan kings, lying brothel owners, reborn terrorists and even a donkey. So never set limits on where God is at work. Yes, the church is God's primary instrument for the kingdom, but this doesn't mean God is not at work in others. We should be the best collaborators in the world.

Create communities where people can love and be loved. The world is obsessed with sex. The church is obsessed with love. Our deepest longing is not for sex but for love. And there are all kinds of people who have plenty of sex and still long for love, and there are other people who will never have sex their whole lives but who know love and intimacy very well.

Be prochurch, rather than parachurch. Learn from the monastic traditions that every generation needs a reformation. The greatest dissenters become saints, and discontentment is a gift to the church. But discontentment must lead us to engage, not disengage. Plant communities, not churches. There is only one church. Plant missional communities; become part of the congregations in the neighborhood. Restore them. Let us also rethink things like the tithe and professionalized clergy—and remember what the church was meant to be. Remember that the best critique of what is wrong is the practice of something better. So let's stop complaining about the church we've seen and work on becoming the church that we dream of.

Pray and act. Pray like crazy. Don't let prayer be an excuse for inaction. So often we wait on God while God is waiting on us. Remember the feeding of the fish and loaves. It was a divine conspiracy of God doing something miraculous with us. God doesn't want to change the world without you. But you can't change the world without God. It takes your fish *and* it takes God's miracle. Won't it be a beautiful day when the justice and compassion crowd meet up with prayer and signs and wonders! Christ and the Spirit are one—so following Christ and being filled with the Spirit must be one. May we be one as God is one.

Rethink sin. Sin is when we fall short of what love demands of us. God hates sin, not because we are breaking random laws but because it hurts us, and God can't stand to watch us hurt ourselves. Be quick to judge yourself and slow to judge others. Jesus never said hate sin, love the sinner. Jesus said, love the sinner and hate the sin in you. Let God judge. Let the Spirit convict. Let us love.

Practice confession. Confession is healing and contagious (as is finger-pointing). There is much collateral damage from sex scandals and cover-up bishops, fraudulent televangelists and fallen preachers. People don't expect Christians to be perfect, but they do expect us to be honest. And that is the tragedy—we have not been honest. Imagine a church where people ask for forgiveness before they get caught. Imagine a church where the world sees and hears Christians confess their own imperfections—maybe then they would see that Christ came not for the healthy but for the sick.

Fall in love with Jesus again. Remember this is a divine romance. Wake up in the morning and adore the One you love. Fall asleep at night in the arms of your sweet Savior. Listen to the whisper that you are beloved. Smell incense like God's perfume, and see the saints as God flirting with us, dropping a handkerchief, as it has been said, so that we might smell God's aroma. Cling to Jesus, not simply as Lord but as Lover.

In the name of the Father, Son and Holy Spirit. Amen.

You Had Me at Hello
(Reprise)

Janell Anema

Dear Church,

There is a problem with these letters to you; the problem being that now I know that I am the church. I'm putting aside the stocking-footed, stained-glass idealism of my youth when I thought the church had a steeple and a pastor had the answers. The problem in writing this letter to you is that any counsel, any prophetic word, any encouragement I offer has to be directed first to me. These letters have been for the church, yes, but these messages are for me.

Dear Church,

Thank you. Thank you so much. Tonight, for the first time, I didn't feel alone in the midst of a service, in the midst of worship. All too often I tire when I feel as though I am pressing into the throne room alone. I know that I always have access to the Father, but sometimes I need to commune with you all as I commune with him. Tonight I did. I felt connected to you, church. I felt the pulse of the

Spirit in my own chest, and I was aware of how your breaths seemed to finally match my own. We inhaled—the fragrance of Christ. We exhaled—the stench of our corporate sin. Breathed in—the fullness of life. Breathed out—the death of our nature. In—Jesus. Out—self. We were thirsty tonight, weren't we? I felt his favor. I felt Poppa's delight. Did you?

I can't wait to be with you all again.

Dear Church, Dearest Church,

I have been unraveled by the mysteries and the complexities and the tragic beauties of this relationship, and I am tossed. I am wrecked. I am completely undone and in love with my Jesus. This man—Poppa, Lord, Counselor, Healer, King—is not who I thought he was, not who you taught me he was. Do you know him? Church, you had me hello, and I love you, but I want more for us now. I want more life. I want more mercy. I want rivers of justice that flow from the throne whose waters quench the thirst of trees whose leaves offer healing to the nations. I want revelation. I want heaven here. I want the kingdom come.

Dear Church, dearest Church: we are living in this extended season of Advent, and we should be waiting with expectation, but we seem to be waiting with bated breath and thereby forgetting to live. Don't be afraid to exhale. Don't be afraid to settle into the time and place that he has timed and placed us. Don't be afraid to get your hands dirty. You are dirty. And he loves us.

Dear Church, dearest Church: you whom I love and long for, you my jewel and my crown. Where you go, I will go. Your people will be my people, and where you are buried, I will be buried. But today we are alive. Don't be afraid. I implore you. I beg of you. This land has nothing for you. He is making all things new, and yet we are continually enthralled with mud pies in the slums when he has clearly invited us to a holiday at sea. Don't you know what he has for us? What he has for us today?

Dear Church, dearest Church: I don't have a formula. There is no plan. But there is a wedding, and we are engaged. We are the beloved. What if, instead of adorning our bodies and our bookshelves with the tattoos and the T-shirts and manifestos that point to God, we write his words on our hearts and we live. We submit. We choose. How many times do we forgive? One more time. How many hours do we long after him? One more hour. Which moments do we yield? The next moment. And then the next after that. Because he asks that of me and he asks that of you. Not because it brings people to the pews. And not because it keeps Pastor from moral failure. Not because it makes us right. But because those choices cause us to live as a church engaged, and not as a church estranged.

Dear Church, Dearest Church: you had me at hello. I love you.

Appendix

Letters to a Future Church
from the End of a Millennium

Some years ago *Christianity Today* imagined a project similar to our Eighth Letter conference. Several leaders of the church were invited to draft "letters Jesus might write to churches today"; they were reprinted in the October 25, 1999, issue under the title "You've Got Mail." Here are some of the letters they received, reprinted here with their permission.

To the Church Which Seeks Seekers,

These are the words of the Seeker after lost sheep and lost
   coins and prodigal sons and daughters:
I love your heart for lost people.
I love the way you think and risk and give and stop at nothing
   to let all persons know they matter to me.
I love the way you have reclaimed the task of evangelism for
   the church.
That's just the heart of a shepherd searching for lost sheep; a
   father longing for his lost son.
I love your heart.
I love your devotion to community.
I love to see you gathered in homes to pray and learn and
   grow.

I love how you want everyone to discover the gifts I've given
   them.
I love your activistic spirit; I love to see your service to the
   church, to the city, to the whole world.
I love your passion, your creativity, your desire to see the
   church flourish and prevail.
But I give you two warnings:
First, never stop dreaming big dreams.
The day you get content and sit on your laurels or begin to
   look backward is the day the dream begins to die.
I have such plans for you, if you will only trust me, and not
   stop dreaming.
Second, stay humble.
Remember that I have said: not by might, not by power, but by
   my spirit.
Remember as you enjoy this season of extraordinary
   fruitfulness, I also work in hidden and obscure places as
   well.
Remember that my work is not ultimately about method or
   technique.
Remember to cherish deep thought and careful study as well
   as bold action.
Remember that what you do you do through my strength and
   in my name.
Stay humble.
To the one who overcomes, I will give a place in that
   community where finally all seeking will be done; where all
   lost sheep and lost coins and lost people will finally, fully
   be found.

Imagined by John Ortberg

To the Church Called Mainline:

Behold I make all things new! Even you.

How eagerly you began the twentieth century, which you so confidently called "Christian." You organized to beat the devil, to build, to expand, to crusade, to reform, to grow. Quite a contrast to the way your century ended. You, who enjoyed thinking of yourselves as "mainline," got sidelined. Though you are averse to taking my Word literally, for my sake, and for yours, I hope that you will at least take these words seriously.

I, the One who so exuberantly turned water into wine at Cana, tire of your propensity to turn wine into water at your bureaucracies in Nashville, Minneapolis, and Louisville. The best thing about you is your past. What does that tell you? My, how you loved to organize and build! You made North America into the most thoroughly Protestant Christian place in the world. Hospitals, orphanages, schools, nursing homes, printing presses. You really took love of neighbor to a new level, and I'm grateful. And while I enjoyed dismantling sacred edifices rather than building them, you built some beautiful churches. Give me *The Lutheran Hymnal* any day over most of those tasteless "praise choruses" of some of my evangelical friends.

Fosdick, Harkness, Peale, Steimlie, Thurman, Achtemeier can preach for me any time they like. I wish some of them would steer a bit closer to the Scriptures, but I'll speak to them individually about that. When you mainliners stop talking about me, your preaching tends to get moralistic and trite. I hate that. It wouldn't kill you to get back to the Bible.

You know me, I love to make the oldline new. If you will stick with me, I shall give you a future, new wineskins, and all that. I am Lord of Life, not death. I shall move you from mordant decline to life. I've still got plans for you. You'll be smaller, but small can be good. Ask the Mennonites. You will no longer be in charge of the nation, if you ever were. Remember, the national church thing was your idea of church, not mine. Get back to the basics like worship, service, and witness. Don't mourn the downsizing of your bureaucracy. You were once good at mission. Now that much of North America has never heard of me, it's about time to start thinking of yourselves as missionaries.

Your marginalization may prove to be providential. I promise you renewal, not restoration. Many will be grateful for your mainline openhandedness, the way you manage to make room for such a wide range of faithfulness within your congregations, your confidence that the church is more than an isolated congregation, that I ought to have a Body, and that the witness of the Saints is worth celebrating today.

Personally, I think you tend to be open-minded to a fault. Latitudinarianism is you all over. I wish you would hire some theologians with some guts for a change. Can't you find something more fun to do than General Assemblies, General Conferences, and Diocesan Conventions? Some of your good ideas from the last century may need a decent burial if I can work birth in you in the next.

One more thing. Please get out of the middle of the road! That's where all the accidents happen, theologically speaking. Remember, I wasn't crucified for my moderation.

Imagined by William H. Willimon

To the Inner-City Pastor and Church:

From him who was rich beyond all measure but became poor for your sake.

You must never succumb to the notion that Christianity in its earliest and purest expression was addressed to the affluent, the well-situated, the so-called movers and shakers of the society.

The Christian faith has been appropriated and tailored by the privileged. This is not all bad, since it is part of the inspired genius of the faith to fit all circumstances of the human condition. This ought not to obscure the truth that the Christian faith began among the disallowed and rejects of the empire of the Caesars, who lived in the back alleys of need and the ghettos of poverty in the cities and villages of the Greco-Roman world.

Therefore, you who preach to marginalized people, whether in the teeming cities of America or the poverty-stricken environs of Appalachia, must declare that the kingdoms of this world are not final and are not favored by God. I said it and you must preach it, "Blessed be ye poor: for yours is the kingdom of God." Therefore, the Spirit of the Lord is upon you, as it was upon me, to preach the gospel to the poor. To do so is not to say that the privileged are shut out, since "with God all things are possible." Probable? That is another matter.

You must not forget that "he which hath the sharp sword with two edges" has "a few things against thee." The poor, those who are most easily exploited, are at the mercy of those who come in my name. This is because religious faith is so precious, and only precious things can be prostituted. You must never forget Simon the magician who wanted to mix the manifestation of the power of the Holy Spirit with the power of money. He was told that he was "in the gall of bitterness, and in the bond of iniquity" (Acts 8:23).

There are shysters, shills, and confidence people posing as

ministers of religion, glutting the television screens with their bizarre clothing, their vulgar jewelry, their preoccupation with sexual innuendoes, their sleazy sales pitches—all designed to prey on poor, gullible people. They are the counterpart in the inner city of those merchants of hatred in the majority community who cloak their racism in a shabby piosity and fake emotions. All are reincarnations of Simon the sorcerer—who saw religions as a tool by which to dupe the poor and susceptible. Always, "shun profane and vain babblings: for they will increase unto more ungodliness" (2 Timothy 2:16).

As the first Galahads of the Cross used the Roman highways to spread the gospel, though they were built for different reasons, so you must make the circumstances in which you and your people live serve my cause. You live in a capitalistic society. Make it serve me, whatever the intentions might be of those who are its economic royalists.

In my name, every Christian church in the inner cities of America ought to develop an endowment fund for community redemption and renewal. Make money for the kingdom of God. Let the interest from these funds, in my name, reach out to the least of my brothers and sisters. Never forget in all we do that we are to be judged at last not by creeds or crowds, not by buildings or budgets, but by the one who says that in those we count the lowliest and the least, it was really *I* who was "hungry" and "thirsty," "a stranger," "naked," and "in prison."

Through it all, like a master theme, in your preaching and practice, by lip and by life, there ought to sound the saints' glad, grateful, grand refrain: "For thou wast slain, and hast redeemed us to God by Thy blood out of every kindred, and tongue, and people, and nation; and hast made us unto our God kings and priests: and we shall reign . . ." Forever!

Imagined by Gardner Taylor

To the Suburban Church of North America

A message from the Son of God, Jesus, whom you call Master and who calls you to follow him.

My churches in suburbia are one of the wonders of the world—there has never been anything quite like them. What energy, enthusiasm, generosity! And you're honest. Hypocrisy has always been a big problem for me, and I don't expect ever to eradicate it, but it is not conspicuous among you. Of all forms of pretense, religious pretense is the worst. Thankfully, I don't find many pretenders among you.

But I do have this against you: you're far too impressed with Size and Power and Influence. You are impatient with the small and the slow. You exercise little discernment between the ways of the world and my ways. It distresses me that you so uncritically copy the attitudes and methods that make your life in suburbia work so well. You grab onto anything that works and looks good. You do so many good things, but too often you do them in the world's way instead of mine, and so seriously compromise your obedience.

I understand why, for most of you have gotten along pretty well in the world—you're well-educated, well-housed, well-paid, well-thought-of; it's only natural that you should put the values and methods that have worked so well for you into service for me. But don't you realize that however successful these attitudes and methods have been in achieving American benefits, it has come at a terrible price: depersonalizing people into functions; turning virtually everything into a cause or commodity to be used or fixed or consumed, doing everything you can to keep suffering at arm's length? The suburban church has a lot of people in it, it functions very well, you can make almost anything happen. But honestly, now, do you think that this is what I had in mind when I said, "Follow me," and then headed for Golgotha in Jerusalem?

Here's what I want you to do. I want you to start off the new millennium by purging your imagination of your suburban assumptions. I want you to do it by spending the next couple of years reading carefully and repeatedly the sixteen Hebrew prophets, Isaiah to Malachi. I have used these prophets over and over again through the centuries to separate my people from the cultures in which they lived. They are one of my standard ways of putting my people back on the path of simple faith and obedience and worship in defiance of all that the world admires and rewards. My Spirit continues to use these prophets to train my people in discerning the difference between the ways of the world and the ways of the gospel. He wants to use them with you.

To the church that not only believes what I say but follows me in the way I do it, I'll give a simple, uncluttered life that is hospitable to the wanderers and misguided, the hurried and harried men and women of this world. I want to use you to give them a taste of sabbath and heaven.

Are you listening? Really listening?

Imagined by Eugene Peterson

Thank You

A book like this doesn't happen without numerous people and organizations cheering us along. Epiphaneia would like to thank Winston Ling, Brian Stiller and George Sweetman, among many others at Tyndale University College and Seminary for their support, encouragement and wisdom. They have proven to us time and again that they believed in what God was doing through Epiphaneia and continually helped us to accomplish those things. We couldn't have asked for a better place to spend such formative years.

We'd also like to thank Mark Peterson at Bridgeway Foundation and Word Made Flesh, Deb Tempelmeyer at David C. Cook, Geri Rodman at Inter-Varsity Christian Fellowship, David Bronkema and Sharon Gramby-Sobukwe at Eastern University, Kevin Kirk at McMaster Divinity School, Willard Metzger at World Vision and Jeff Steckley with the Mennonite Church Eastern Canada. This book would simply not exist without your support!

We've had a few volunteers who have helped at almost all of our events, and we're so grateful to them. Thank you, Craig Bertrim, Tracy Bertrim, Chris Clements, Nyssa Clements, Rachel Colquhoun, Christina Cox, Tim Cruikshank, Michelle Hodgson, Jason Locke, Catherine Locke, Joe Manafo, Jason Penney, Danielle Rourke, Dan Slade, Pat Sutherland, Alicia Wilson and Siobhan Wilson. Thank you!

We'd also like to thank Dave Zimmerman at InterVarsity Press for believing in this project and helping it arrive at a better publishing home than we could have ever imagined.

Finally, thanks to our families and friends. We're grateful to God for each of you.

Notes

[1]Anthony Dworkin, "The Case for Minor Utopias," *Prospect*, July 2007, p. 43.

[2]Oscar Wilde, "What Is a Cynic? A Man Who Knows the Price of Everything and the Value of Nothing," *Lady Windermere's Fan* (1892).

[3]Conflicting values, tensions, paradoxes and dilemmas are different ways this phenomena is talked about by various authors. This phenomena has been thoroughly studied by Dr. Barry Johnson. See his work called Polarity Management at www.polaritymanagement.com.

[4]Richard E. Nisbett and Theodore D. Wilson, "Telling More Than We Can Know: Verbal Reports on Mental Processes," *Psychological Review* 84 (1977): 231-59.

[5]Elliot Aronson and Carol Travis, *Mistakes Were Made (But Not By Me)* (New York: Harcourt, 2007).

[6]See chapter one of my *Scandal of the Evangelical Conscience* (Grand Rapids: Baker, 2005).

Contributors

 Janell Anema is a waitress, a professor, a former church secretary, and an avid vacationer who recently relocated to Philadelphia, Pennsylvania. From the mountains of Colorado to the villages of Liberia, Janell has spent the last five years living the dream and learning how to write about it. She hopes to continually integrate her passions for travel, the Lord, his people and the church as she seeks to love God and love people in Kensington, in Kenya and in other communities around the world. Janell is a wordsmith, a wanderer, a lover of people, a lover of places. And a member of churches.

 Tim Arnold spent a decade of leading a team-building company that worked with corporate clients, government organizations and the United Nations. Now Tim is the outreach pastor at Southridge (www.southridge.cc), a very unique local church that has a 35-bed homeless shelter located in its church facility.

Kester Brewin is a part-time teacher and writer on theology, technology education and pretty much anything else. He's also a consultant for BBC Education and has published regularly around issues in secondary education. In 2004 his first book, *The Complex Christ,* was published and has also been released in the U.S. under the title *Signs of Emergence.* In 2010 *Other: Loving Self, God and Neighbour in a World of Fractures* was published. He's currently working on a book about pirates and a novel based on Steinbeck's *Cannery Row,* set in a seaside village in Essex.

Walter Brueggemann is Professor Emeritus at Columbia Theological Seminary. He is an ordained minister in the United Church of Christ and a past president of the Society of Biblical Literature. He has recently published a collection of his sermons at Westminster John Knox Press.

Tim Challies is a follower of Jesus Christ, a husband to Aileen and a father to three young children. He worships and serves as a pastor at Grace Fellowship Church in Toronto, Ontario, edits Discerning Reader and is a cofounder of Cruciform Press.

Shane Claiborne a founding partner of The Simple Way, a faith community in inner-city Philadelphia that has helped to birth and connect radical faith communities around the world. Shane writes and travels extensively, speaking about peacemaking, social justice and Jesus. He is featured in the DVD series *Another World Is Possible*, and is the author of several books, including *The Irresistible Revolution, Jesus for President* and *Becoming the Answer to Our Prayers*.

Nathan Colquhoun lives in Sarnia, Ontario, with his wife, Rachel, where he coleads a church called the Story and coruns a media company called Storyboard Solutions. He blogs at nathancolquhoun .com.

Andy Crouch is special assistant to the president at Christianity Today International and the author of *Culture Making: Recovering Our Creative Calling*. He lives in Swarthmore, Pennsylvania.

Kathy Escobar copastors The Refuge, an eclectic faith community in North Denver dedicated to those on the margins of life and faith. A spiritual director, writer and speaker, Kathy's newest book is *Down We Go: Living into the Wild Ways of Jesus* (Civitas Press, 2011) and centers on practical ways to cultivate intentional missional community. She lives in Arvada, Colorado, with her husband and five kids, and blogs regularly

Rachel Held Evans is a skeptic and Christ-follower from Dayton, Tennessee—home of the famous Scopes Monkey Trial of 1925. She is the author of *Evolving in Monkey Town: How a Girl Who Knew All the Answers Learned to Ask the Questions* (Zondervan, 2010) and a forthcoming title about her "year of biblical womanhood" in which she followed all of the Bible's commandments for women as literally as possible. She blogs at rachelheldevans.com.

David Fitch is a pastor/church planter/activist in the missional church movement. He is also the B. R. Lindner Professor of Evangelical Theology at Northern Seminary in Chicago. He is author of several books, including *The End of Evangelicalism?* and the forthcoming *Prodigal Christianity: 10 Signposts to the Missional Frontier* (Jossey-Bass, 2013)

Makoto Fujimura is an internationally exhibited artist, the author of two books and numerous essays, a much sought-after speaker, and an art advocate who is recognized worldwide as a cultural influencer by both faith-based and secular media. He aims to bring together people of all backgrounds in conversation and meditation on culture, art and humanity. Fujimura has been a presidential appointee to the National Council on the Arts (2003-2009), has painted live on Carnegie Hall's legendary stage alongside percussionist Susie Ibarra, and founded the International Arts Movement in 1992.

Wendy Gritter has served to build bridges of peace, generosity and respect in the LGBT community and the church through the ministry of New Direction since 2002. A D.Min. candidate, Wendy's research focus is the process of building congregational unity in the midst of diversity and disputable matters. She blogs at www.btgproject.blogspot.com.

Cyril Guérette (aka ILL SEER) is senior pastor of FreeChurch Toronto and associate professor of philosophy and theology at Heritage Baptist College. After receiving his master of philosophy in theology at the University of Cambridge, he is currently completing his Ph.D. at Toronto School of Theology, focusing on the poetic/dialectic nature of St. Anselm's writing. The founder of indie record label PropheticPoetic.com, Cyr has been performing and recording hip-hop music internationally for over a decade, being nominated for a Canadian Gospel Music Award, and has been creating poetry for longer still.

Sarah Lance lives and works among women who have been sexually exploited in Kolkata, India. In 2006 Sarah and fellow community member Kristin Keen cofounded Sari Bari, a social business, to give freedom to women from the sex trade through alternative employment. She continues to dream for things that she may never see and loves sharing life with her Word Made Flesh community, her friends at Sari Bari and the women who continue in bondage in lanes of the red-light area.

Ikenna Onyegbula is a member of The Recipe, a supergroup of spoken word. Harnessing an uncommon amount of beauty and strength on stage while challenging audiences to engage with a vast spectrum of emotions and topics, The Recipe is taking spoken word to new levels. After being crowned Canadian national champs in 2009, team members Ian Keteku, Poetic Speed, OpenSecret and Brandon Wint formed The Recipe to keep their raw energy and mind-blowing collaborations going. They have shared the stage with some of the most profound names in spoken word and music.

 Soong-Chan Rah is the Milton B. Engebretson Associate Professor of Church Growth and Evangelism at North Park Theological Seminary. He is the author of *The Next Evangelicalism* (InterVarsity Press, 2009) and *Many Colors* (Moody Press, 2010).

 Peter Rollins is a widely sought-after writer, lecturer, storyteller and public speaker. He is also the founder of ikon, a faith group that has gained an international reputation for blending live music, visual imagery, soundscapes, theater, ritual and reflection to create what they call "transformance art." Peter gained his higher education from Queens University, Belfast, and has earned degrees (with distinction) in scholastic philosophy (B.A. Hons.), political theory (M.A.) and post-structural thought (Ph.D.). He is currently a research associate with the Irish School of Ecumenics in Trinity College, Dublin, and is the author of the muc-h talked about *How (Not) to Speak of God.* He was born in Belfast but currently resides in Greenwich, Connecticut.

 James Shelly decided to leave church work after fourteen years in ministry to invest more time in the community at large. He is currently a street-level social worker with the Canadian Mental Health Association and a fitness instructor with

GoodLife. He is also an avid blogger and something
of a freelance philosopher. He and his wife, Michelle, are based in London, Ontario.

 Ronald J. Sider (Ph.D., Yale) is professor of theology, holistic ministry and public policy and director of the Sider Center on Ministry and Public Policy at Palmer Theological Seminary, and president
of Evangelicals for Social Action. Sider has spoken
on six continents and published over thirty-one
books, including *Rich Christians in an Age of Hunger*, which was recognized by *Christianity Today* as
one of the one hundred most influential religious
books of the twentieth century and was named the
seventh most influential book in the evangelical
world in the last fifty years.

 Aileen Van Ginkel acts as vice president, Ministry
Services, at The Evangelical Fellowship of Canada.
She has training and wide experience in facilitat-
ing group communications and in partnership development. She is currently engaged in a doctor of
ministry program at Tyndale Seminary, where she
is researching various practices around "communal discernment." Aileen and her husband, Ed-
ward, parent three children, currently aged 25, 23
and 20.

 **Jonathan Wilson-Hartgrove** is a leader of the new
monastic movement and cofounded the Rutba
House community in Durham, North Carolina. An
associate minister at St. John's Baptist Church in
Durham, he also directs the School for Conversion,

a partnership among new monastic communities for alternative theological education. *He is the author of God's Economy, The Wisdom of Stability and,* most recently, *Common Prayer: A Liturgy for Ordinary Radicals.* www.jonathanwilsonhartgrove.com

Sponsors

Before *Letters to a Future Church* was a book, it was a conference. Hosted by the Epiphaneia Network, Eighth Letter was made possible by the following sponsors.

TYNDALE www.tyndale.ca

Tyndale is a transdenominational, evangelical university college and seminary that prepares leaders for the ministry, marketplace and global mission of the church. Tyndale offers a variety of degree programs in a wide range of disciplines and fully accredited programs at both the undergraduate and graduate levels.

David Cook www.davidccook.ca

David C. Cook exists for the sole purpose of equipping grassroots pastors, local church leaders, families and children throughout the world with all the vital discipleship resources they need, translated and culturalized into their own languages.

 www.ivcf.ca

Being shaped by God's word and led by the Holy Spirit, the purpose of Inter-Varsity Christian

Fellowship of Canada is the transformation of youth, students and graduates, in all their ethnic diversity, into fully committed followers of Jesus Christ.

www.bridgewayfoundation.ca

Since its inception, Bridgeway has supported nonprofit organizations that bring transformation to communities around the world. Humbled by Jesus' life, Bridgeway Foundation envisions a bold philanthropy that stretches the ability of people and organizations to learn and serve at the margins.

www.wordmadeflesh.org

Word Made Flesh (WMF) is called and committed to serve Jesus among the most vulnerable of the world's poor. This calling is realized as a prophetic ministry for, and an incarnational, holistic mission among, the poor. WMF focuses its energy to make Jesus known among the poor while reconciling the church with the poor.

www.mcec.ca

The Mennonite Church Eastern Canada's mission is to extend the peace of Jesus Christ, making disciples, growing congregations and forming leaders.

www.worldvision.ca

World Vision is a Christian relief, development and advocacy organization dedicated to working with children, families and communities to overcome poverty and injustice. As followers of Jesus, World Vision is motivated by God's love for all people regardless of race, religion, gender or ethnicity.

www.macdiv.ca

As a community of faith, McMaster Divinity College seeks to be a spiritually and theologically vital and trusted community engaged in the education of those qualified for spiritual leadership in the church.

www.eastern.edu/sld

Eastern University is a Christian university dedicated to the preparation of undergraduate, theological and graduate students for thoughtful and productive lives of Christian faith, leadership and service. The mission is confirmed and celebrated when graduates believe their way into knowledgeable action that influences their world in substantive ways.